MODERN WORLD NATIONS

AFGHANISTAN	IRAN
ARGENTINA	IRAQ
AUSTRALIA	IRELAND
AUSTRIA	ISRAEL
BAHRAIN	ITALY
BERMUDA	JAPAN
BOLIVIA	KAZAKHSTAN
BRAZIL	KENYA
CANADA	KUWAIT
CHINA	MEXICO
COSTA RICA	THE NETHERLANDS
CROATIA	NEW ZEALAND
CUBA	NIGERIA
EGYPT	NORTH KOREA
ENGLAND	NORWAY
ETHIOPIA	PAKISTAN
FRANCE	PERU
REPUBLIC OF GEORGIA	RUSSIA
GERMANY	SAUDI ARABIA
GHANA	SCOTLAND
GUATEMALA	SOUTH AFRICA
ICELAND	SOUTH KOREA
INDIA	UKRAINE

MODERN WORLD NATIONS

Guatemala

Roger E. Dendinger
South Dakota School of Mines and Technology

Series Consulting Editor
Charles F. Gritzner
South Dakota State University

CHELSEA HOUSE
PUBLISHERS
A Haights Cross Communications Company

Philadelphia

Frontispiece: Flag of Guatemala

Cover: Village of Solola, Guatemala

CHELSEA HOUSE PUBLISHERS

VP, NEW PRODUCT DEVELOPMENT Sally Cheney
DIRECTOR OF PRODUCTION Kim Shinners
CREATIVE MANAGER Takeshi Takahashi
MANUFACTURING MANAGER Diann Grasse

Staff for GUATEMALA

EXECUTIVE EDITOR Lee Marcott
PRODUCTION EDITOR Megan Emery
PICTURE RESEARCHER 21st Century Publishing and Communications, Inc.
COVER DESIGNER Keith Trego
SERIES DESIGNER Takeshi Takahashi
LAYOUT 21st Century Publishing and Communications, Inc.

A Haights Cross Communications ↗ Company

http://www.chelseahouse.com

First Printing

1 3 5 7 9 8 6 4 2

Library of Congress Cataloging-in-Publication Data

Dendinger, Roger.
  Guatemala/by Roger E. Dendinger.
    p. cm.—(Modern world nations)
Includes index.
Summary: Describes the history, geography, government, economy, people, and culture
of Guatemala.
  ISBN 0-7910-7477-3
  1. Guatemala—Juvenile literature. [1. Guatemala.] I. Title. II. Series.
F1463.2.D46 2003
972.81—dc22

                                                                2003014160

Table of Contents

1 Introducing Guatemala   9

2 Natural Landscapes   13

3 Guatemala Through Time   31

4 People and Culture   47

5 Government   63

6 Economy   75

7 Living in Guatemala Today –
Regional Contrasts   85

8 Looking Ahead   95

Facts at a Glance   102
History at a Glance   104
Bibliography   106
Index   107

Guatemala

A Mayan trader and her daughter watch the sun set from the shore of Lake Atitlán in the town of Panajachel. British writer Aldous Huxley visited Atitlán in the 1930s and described it as "the most beautiful place on earth."

Introducing Guatemala

"The land where the rainbow begins." This is how the traditional Mayan people of Guatemala describe their country. A land of striking and sometimes violent contrasts, Guatemala's vivid colors reflect a varied land and a people with ancient roots.

The colors of this land are echoed in the hues of *traje*, the traditional costume of the Mayans. Ancient and contemporary weavers dye their hand-woven cotton the same dark orange and red tones as molten lava from the country's volcanoes. Luxuriant greens of the rain forest are duplicated in depictions of the Resplendent Quetzal. The iridescent green, red, and white feathers of this tropical bird have symbolized the land since ancient times.

Other depictions of ancient life and symbols use the blue of Lake Atitlán, a mountain lake that English author Aldous Huxley called the most beautiful place in the world. Outside the spectrum of rainbow colors are found the black volcanic sands of the Pacific coast and the bleached chalk white colors of the lost cities of the Maya.

So close to North America, yet so distant in many ways, Guatemala is home both to modern culture and to one of the world's most ancient civilizations. The effects of globalization and reverence for the ancient god Quetzalcoatl coexist somewhat uncomfortably here.

Its natural beauty and cultural richness are appealing, but Guatemala has another face as well. It is a place of recent civil war and ongoing political and economic turmoil. Ethnic bitterness and social inequality are not uncommon. Ruled by military dictatorships for most of the past hundred years, the country only now is transitioning from repressive tyranny to uneasy democracy.

Guatemala is one of the original "banana republics," a derisive term for Central American countries long dependent on agricultural exports to the United States. It is a fact that much of the country's infrastructure—its railroad, telegraph lines, and ports—was built and controlled by U.S. interests, principally the United Fruit Company. Like its Mayan heritage, this aspect of the country's past is still alive as well. Despite economic advances of the last five years, Guatemala is still dependent on banana, coffee, and sugarcane production for most of its export revenue.

With more than 13 million people, Guatemala is the largest state in Central America, and its population is growing the fastest. Only in Bolivia, a central Andean country in South America, is a larger share of the people full-blood Amerindian (Native Americans of North and South America). Although Mayans make up more than half the population, the *ladinos* dominate the country politically and economically. Ladinos are people of Spanish and mixed blood ancestry who are European in culture. The culture gap between them and the rural Mayans is vast.

What can an outsider make of such a place? To begin with, an understanding of the traditions of the Mayan people is important. So, too, is examining the economics of development. Joining the world community of trade and competition may be necessary if Guatemala is to reconcile itself with its bloody past and live

Guatemala is located approximately in the middle of the Central American land bridge that connects North and South America. It is the largest state in Central America and its population is growing the fastest.

up to the potential of its beautiful land and people. Two themes, then, will guide us through the "land where the rainbow begins"—tradition, and its opposite, modernism.

Guatemala has coastline on both its west and east sides. On the west is the Pacific Ocean and on the east is the Caribbean Sea. This view is from Livingston, which lies on the east coast.

2

Natural Landscapes

Guatemala is located approximately in the middle of the Central American isthmus, the narrow land bridge that connects North and South America, then widens into the flat limestone tablelands of the Yucatán Peninsula.

Formed in the late Pliocene (about 2.5 to 3 million years ago) by a shift in the Caribbean tectonic plate, the Central American or Mesoamerican land bridge linked the two great landmasses of the Western Hemisphere at a crucial time in evolutionary development. During this epoch, plant and animal species were on the move, migrating north and south over the narrow strip of land. In places only 80 miles (130 kilometers) wide, the isthmus acted as a biological filter for this migration, selecting some species for passage and acting as a barrier to others. As a result, Central America is a region where exotics from both north and south mingle.

Guatemala lies entirely within the tropics, between 14 and 18 degrees north latitude. Bordered by Mexico on the north and west, the country also shares political boundaries with Honduras and El Salvador on the southeast. A rugged northeast border with Belize, formerly British Honduras, has been contested bitterly over the years. Some Guatemalans continue to claim that the territory belonging to Belize is rightfully theirs. The problem is so intense that the United Kingdom maintains a small contingent of marines in a tropical forest base in Belize.

Tropical settings are defined by their proximity to the equator where the length of daylight does not vary much throughout the year. Nevertheless, dramatic differences in local microclimates make it difficult to generalize about the country's weather. Within an area slightly larger than the state of Tennessee, Guatemala's natural landscapes range from dense forests in the north to cool mountain peaks in the south-central mountainous region, to seasonally dry savanna grasslands on the Pacific coast.

CLIMATE AND ALTITUDINAL ZONES

To make sense of the variety of local physical conditions in Guatemala, one must look at topography, or differences in elevation. Geographers define variations in tropical subregions by the physical characteristics determined by elevation. Altitudinal zonation is a way to understand local variations in temperature, humidity, and vegetation that characterize much of Central America.

Some subregions of Guatemala have cool weather during certain seasons, and even cold weather occurs in some places. But, as in much of Central America, elevation is the main determinant of temperature rather than seasonal shifts of sun angle. Altitudinal zones are measured somewhat differently from region to region in Central and South America, although from Mexico to Brazil the same names are applied to these zones.

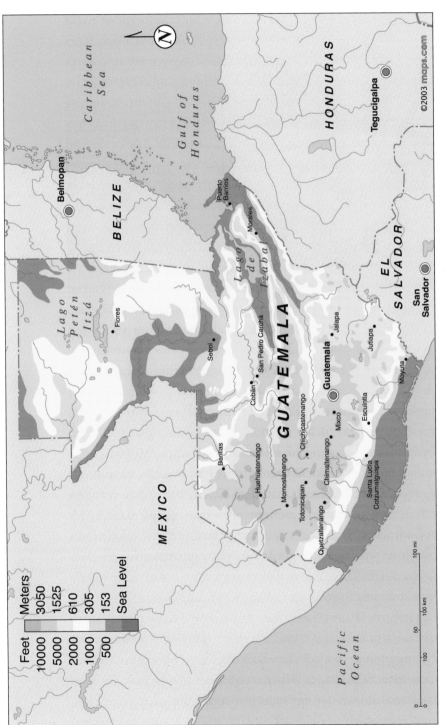

Guatemala is bordered by Mexico on the north and west, Belize on the north and east, and also shares boundaries with Honduras and El Salvador on the southeast. The variety of local physical conditions in Guatemala is due to the differences in elevation. The four zones common to South America are *tierra caliente, tierra templada, tierra fría,* and *tierra helado.*

The Motagua River on its way to the Gulf of Honduras flows through a wide valley north of Zacapa. Here, tierra caliente meets tierra templada.

The four zones common to Central America are *tierra caliente, tierra templada, tierra fria,* and *tierra helado.*

The tierra caliente (literally "hot land") extends from sea level upward to 2,500 feet (750 meters). In these low-lying areas, ample year-round sunlight and humidity create a consistently warm, and usually very wet, environment. As in other parts of Central America, plantation agriculture often is found in this zone. Guatemala's banana and sugarcane plantations are in the lowlands, both on the Caribbean and the Pacific coasts. Like other places in Central America, settlement came late to the lowlands. Guatemala's tierra caliente was very lightly populated until the development of banana plantations in the early twentieth century.

In the "temperate land," the tierra templada, temperatures are more moderate. At 2,500–6,000 feet (760–1,800 meters) above elevation, the templada is warm, although cool temperatures are common at night. At this elevation, some wheat and corn are raised for subsistence, but this zone's traditional

San Antonio Aguas Calientes is a highland village in an upland basin in the tierra templada. This town is famous for its traditional weaving styles.

commercial crop is coffee, which thrives in areas with volcanic soils and mild dry seasons. Most of Guatemala's coffee grows on the southern slopes of the Sierra Madre. There, conditions are ideal for such rich varieties as Antigua Guatemala, one of several specialty coffees grown for export.

The tierra fria, or cold land, extends up to the tree line in the mountains, about 12,000 feet (3,600 meters). Beyond this point trees cannot find a purchase in the rocky soils, and cool year-round temperatures make agriculture impossible. In Guatemala, the upper reaches of this zone are sparsely inhabited, although potatoes, barley, and some dairying provide a way of life for hardy mountain dwellers between 6,000 and 9,000 feet (1,820 and 2,740 meters).

Above the tree line lies the "frozen land." The tierra helado, at 12,000 feet (3,600 meters) and up, contains areas of year round snow and ice and poor mountain soils. In portions of highland South America, the tierra helado is used seasonally for grazing, but Guatemala has only a tiny bit of land lying in this uppermost altitudinal zone. Guatemala's highest point is the 13,845-foot (4,220-meter) volcano, Tajumulco.

Tropical climates lack what people in most of North America would call winter conditions. The coolest average monthly temperature is warmer than 64°F (18°C). Tropical climates also are described by variations in rainfall, elevation, and ocean currents. The narrow Pacific coast is hot and wet with a brief dry season. The rest of the country is hot and wet year round, with local variations explained by altitudinal zonation.

Physically, the country divides neatly into four distinct regions: the Pacific lowlands, the highlands, the Petén, and the Caribbean lowlands.

PACIFIC LOWLANDS

The narrow strip of Guatemala's Pacific shoreline at its widest point is only 30 miles (48 kilometers) across. In some places, the southwest slope of the volcanic range approaches to within 10 miles (16 kilometers) of the ocean. This slim band of coastline has no bay or gulf indentations, a disadvantage for attracting ocean-going ships. With no natural harbors, vessels must lie at anchor off the coast at the small ports of Ocos, Champerico, and San Jose. Historically, this disadvantage has meant that much of the country's foreign trade was focused on the eastern, Caribbean coast. Much of the country's sugarcane is produced in the narrow coastal plain.

Although the coast's black sands and unspoiled scenery can be beautiful, strong currents near shore, rip tides, and fierce under-tows make the Pacific a dangerously challenging place to swim. Most beaches are not marked, and uninformed visitors will be in for a surprise if they venture more than a few feet from shore. Shallow lagoons and winding mangrove swamps give the region an exotic and mysterious flavor just inland from the beaches. Most of the rest of the coastal plain is savanna. Seasonally dry, this band of grasslands extends from about 19 degrees north latitude on the Mexican coast south to the border with El Salvador.

HIGHLANDS

Guatemala sits on either side of the great mountain backbone of the Western Hemisphere that runs along the Pacific side of the continent from Alaska to the southern tip of South America, Tierra del Fuego. This mountain backbone is the Continental Divide of the isthmus.

Two major mountain ranges trend west to east across the south-central portion of the country. The headwaters of the Motagua River separate the northern limestone ranges of the Cuchumatanes from the volcanic ridges of the Sierra Madre in the south. Although the Sierra Madre and most of the northern range are very close to the Pacific, almost all the highland region drains into the Caribbean.

Guatemala's portion of the Sierra Madre range contains 32 volcanoes and has been the site of some of the hemisphere's most devastating earthquakes. One of the largest eruptions in the twentieth century was from the Santa Maria volcano in 1902. Several of Guatemala's volcanoes are classed as stratovolcanoes, or composite volcanoes, steep-sided, conical structures topped by bowl-shaped summit craters.

Wherever converging plate boundaries are found, volcanic and seismic (earthquake) activity is common. In Central America, the Pacific "Ring of Fire" is a force that people live with daily. Earthquakes and volcanic eruptions are natural hazards taken for granted by most people throughout Central America, and Guatemala is no exception. From the time of the earliest Amerindian inhabitants to today's modern capital city, the people of this country live with the possibility of deadly quakes and volcanoes. The country's volcanoes picket the backbone of the Sierra Madre, where most of Guatemala's 13 million people live. When Pacaya, Guatemala's most spectacularly active volcano, puts on a fiery display, Guatemala City's 3 million residents have a ringside seat.

Earthquakes are even more feared than volcanoes. Worldwide, most earthquakes occur near the edge of active tectonic plates.

Pressure is released occasionally when fault lines along plate boundaries slip suddenly. In Guatemala, the effects of such slippage can be severe. The deadly 1976 quake that centered in the central Sierra Madre measured 7.5 on the Richter Scale. This killer quake left 22,000 people dead and a million people homeless.

Volcanic eruptions and earthquakes shaped early colonial settlement patterns in Guatemala. The country's first capital was located at a spot now known as Ciudad Vieja—literally, Old Town. On September 11, 1541, shortly after its founding, the capital was destroyed by an earthquake and the resulting mudflow from a nearby volcano. Today, the volcano is called Volcán de Agua, the water volcano, named after the wall of water and mud that destroyed the town.

After the destruction of Ciudad Vieja, a new capital city was built a few miles away at Antigua. In 1773, this settlement also was destroyed by an earthquake. The colonial capital was moved again, this time east to the present site of Guatemala City. Antigua was abandoned but later reinhabited. Today, much of the seventeenth- and eighteenth-century architecture not destroyed in the quake still stands, incorporated into the newer urban fabric of the town.

Most Guatemalans live in or near the mountains. The country's capital, Guatemala City, sits in a mountain basin at about 4,900 feet (1,500 meters). At this elevation, the temperature range is comfortably narrow—between 50 degrees F. (10°C) in winter and 80° (26°C) in summer. Humidity is high year round, but the city enjoys a distinctive wet summer and dry winter pattern.

Other mountain basins between 5,000 and 8,000 feet (1,525 and 2,538 meters) in elevation include Lake Atitlán, which English author Aldous Huxley described as "the most beautiful place on earth." Atitlán's backdrop is composed of three conical stratovolcanoes—Volcán Atitlán and its twin, Tolimán, to the north, and Volcán San Pedro on the south shore. The lake is 5,128 feet (1,563 meters) above sea level and has a depth of 1,049 feet (320 meters). As such, Atitlán qualifies as

Ruins from the 1773 earthquake in the old Spanish capital of Antigua form part of the contemporary fabric of the town. Antigua was abandoned as an administrative center and the colonial capital was moved to Guatemala City. *Volcán de Agua*, or "Water Volcano," looms in the distance.

the deepest lake in the Western Hemisphere. Three other volcanoes are on the lake's southern shore, each more than 10,000 feet (3,050 meters) high. Ringed by volcanoes, Atitlán's prominence among the world's most remarkable sights cannot be overstated. Huxley was right!

CARIBBEAN LOWLANDS

The Caribbean lowlands sit in the eastern tierra caliente. Hot year round and wet most of the year, the lowlands on this side of the country were the last part of Guatemala to be settled. Amerindian natives and early Spanish settlers both preferred the temperate mountains to the energy-sapping humidity of the coast. Puerto Barrios, founded in 1883 as a port for coffee exports, is still Guatemala's largest harbor and most active trans-shipment point for international trade.

Two of the country's major rivers drain into the Caribbean's Gulf of Honduras. The Rio Sarstun, on the border with Belize, drains much of the north central portion of the country. To the southeast, closer to the border with Honduras, is the Rio Motagua, the largest of the lowland valley rivers. The headwaters of the Motagua are high in the volcanic range where rainfall is abundant. As it winds its way to the Caribbean, the river shapes a wide valley in the seasonally dry northeastern portion of the country. Dry lands and beautiful stands of cactus in this part of the Motagua Valley contrast sharply with the lush greenness of the mountains.

PETÉN

Guatemala's Petén region lies in the northern one-third of the country. Sparsely inhabited, it is the site of rapid environmental changes. Guatemala is the only Central American country to possess oil in sufficient amounts to justify drilling. Recently, oil companies have begun road building throughout much of the region. They are in the process of opening up remote lands to subsistence farmers, cattle operations, and other development.

The Petén lies in the central portion of the Yucatan Peninsula, a vast limestone shelf or tableland sitting between 500 and 700 feet (150 and 215 meters) above sea level. Until recently, most of the Petén was covered with dense rain forest. Annual rainfall averages 40-70 inches (1,000-1,800 millimeters).

This region is one of the world's best examples of karst topography. Karst landscapes are formed when carbonic acid dissolves limestone. Carbon dioxide is concentrated in soil, and when water moves through it, carbonic acid is formed. The process also occurs in groundwater, dissolving limestone underground and creating caverns. These caverns often collapse, creating sinkholes, or what in the Yucatán are called *cenotes*.

Northern Petén is home to Guatemala's Maya Biosphere Reserve (MBR), a vast protected area comprising more than 13 percent of the country's territory. This region contains critical

Petén is the location of dozens of ancient Mayan ruins that have not yet been excavated. In the dense vegetation only the tops of the temple ruins at Tikal can be seen poking through the rain forest.

habitat for rare tropical plants and animals. It is also the location of dozens of ancient Mayan ruins that have not yet been excavated. The MBR is part of a worldwide system of endangered environments called the International Network of Biosphere Reserves.

The MBR is also the largest single area of tropical rain forest in Central America. Its 5.1 million acres (2 million hectares) are divided into three distinct land uses. A 1.8-million-acre (750,000-hectare) wilderness area is protected from most forms of development. Another 2.1 million acres (850,000 hectares) are defined as multiple-use lands where indigenous peoples may practice new forms of sustainable agriculture. Surrounding this core of protected lands is a 1.2-million-acre (486,000-hectare) buffer zone comprised of private holdings. Although Guatemala has lost much of its forestlands to traditional slash-and-burn shifting agriculture, sustainable forestry practices are slowly changing traditional subsistence patterns within the MBR and in the forests to the south. Harvesting mahogany and other rare tropical hardwoods is being replaced by harvesting chicle (the basis of chewing gum) and allspice, as well as gathering xate ferns (used in flower arrangements).

Big-leaf mahogany has been harvested in the Petén and in nearby Belize and Mexico since the late nineteenth century. Also called American mahogany, this increasingly rare tropical hardwood is processed into luxury furniture for markets in North America, which imports about 60 percent of the world's mahogany. Long prized for its distinctive color and its strength, American mahogany is one of the world's most expensive woods. And it is becoming more expensive as supplies dwindle and demand remains high. Other species of New World mahogany already are commercially extinct. Deforestation has reduced the range of this species in Central America by approximately two-thirds. Slow growing, the big-leaf variety takes 55 to 120 years to reach maturity. Full grown, it may reach heights of more than 150 feet (46 meters).

Much of the Central American mahogany that reaches world markets is harvested illegally. Environmentalists have tried to stop the trade in big-leaf mahogany through applying the Conference on International Trade in Endangered Species (CITES). Years of effort finally paid off at the annual meeting of CITES in November 2002, where a joint proposal by Guatemala and Nicaragua protecting mahogany was approved. The plan calls for strict controls on the mahogany trade from Latin America.

According to environmentalists, the black market in big-leaf mahogany is a tempting option for people in a region where poverty is widespread. Middlemen pay loggers about $50 for a full-grown tree, and then sell the wood for $1,200 to exporters. The same tree can produce furniture worth about $18,000 in U.S. or European markets. Under the new CITES rules, all international trade in Latin American mahogany must come from sustainable and strictly regulated forests, such as the MBR's multiple-use lands.

Unlike big-leaf mahogany, the chicle or sapodilla tree is common in the Petén. The tree's milky juice, also called chicle, is used in the manufacture of chewing gum and gives it resiliency. Mayans chewed unprocessed chicle. Chicle is collected from living trees by cutting shallow grooves in the bark. The chicle drips out of these grooves into bags or buckets attached under the incisions, and is then boiled and allowed to harden. After it is formed into blocks, it is shipped to the United States where it is processed into chewing gum. Nuts of the tree are also harvested, a sustainable practice in keeping with the goals of preserving the MBR forest.

Another sustainable tropical forest activity centers on the xate palm, a beautiful fast-growing tropical palm. The xate's rich green leaves are cut carefully so as not to damage the plant, bundled, and exported to the United States and Europe, where they are used in ornamental flower arrangements. Xate leaves are especially popular in floral wedding designs.

An increasingly important tropical forest export is allspice. The berries from varieties of the pimento species are harvested, dried over fires or in the sun, boiled, then shipped to the United States and Europe. Allspice is used in sweet pickles, pumpkin pie spices, seafood seasoning, and other culinary preparations.

DEFORESTATION

As in other tropical regions around the world, Guatemala's rain forests are threatened by deforestation. When the forest is cleared, the region has a related problem, laterization, or hardening of the soil. Laterization, in turn, slows or even stops the process of forest rejuvenation. One source of deforestation is the traditional agricultural practice known as slash-and-burn, a land-intensive type of farming that is destroying rain forests in Central and South America, Africa, and Southeast Asia.

In slash-and-burn shifting cultivation, which is a form of subsistence agriculture, a farmer clears a plot of rain forest. Most plots are 3 to 5 acres (1.2 to 2.0 hectares) in size, which is

This landscape shows the results of the conversion of rain forest to farmland through the traditional agricultural slash- and- burn practices.

the maximum area a family can handle. All of the cleared vegetation is burned on site. Burning fixes nitrogen and other minerals in the soil, temporarily boosting soil fertility. Crops such as manioc and yams are planted, and, in the warm, wet, low latitudes, farmers can produce up to three crops a year. The result is that the plot is usually worked year round without a fallow period. After three to six years, the beneficial effects of the burning wear off. Productivity declines, the plot is abandoned, the subsistence family looks for another piece of forest to clear, and the cycle begins again. Cattle ranchers often take up abandoned rainforest land. Grazing cattle strip the fragile landscape of what little vegetative cover it might have, and serious erosion problems develop. If the soil is directly exposed to the high heat and moisture, laterite—brick-like soil—forms.

Traditional subsistence practices were not a problem throughout most of human development because populations were low, land was abundant, and abandoned subsistence plots had time to recover. For the past hundred years, however, populations in the tropics have been growing steadily. As a result, subsistence agriculture threatens to consume the remaining rain forests not only in Guatemala but worldwide. The United Nations Food and Agriculture Organization (FAO) estimates that approximately 0.6 percent of the Earth's rain forests are lost each year to deforestation. Another sobering estimate is that half of the Earth's rain forests have been cut down in the past 50 years. Central America has lost about 85 percent of its rainforest area since the middle of the twentieth century when deforestation began accelerating.

ANIMALS

One of the world's ornithological treasures is a symbol both of Guatemala's Mayan heritage and the country's modern identity. The Resplendent Quetzal, a member of the Trogon family of highly colored tropical birds, is much sought after by photographers, eco-tourists, and bird-watchers alike. This relatively rare dark green and red bird has a compact body, but it sports iridescent green tail feathers up to 24 inches (60 centimeters) long. In flight, these feathers undulate gracefully behind the bird's small delicate body and tufted head.

The Resplendent Quetzal was so revered by the Mayans that killing one was a crime punishable by death. Their tail feathers were used in elaborate headdresses. The Aztecs and Mayans trapped the quetzals, removed their long tail feathers, and set them free to grow new feathers. Today, quetzals are difficult to protect because they move around regionally and their forest habitat is dwindling.

At home in mountain forests, the quetzal houses itself and its brood in the abandoned woodpecker holes of dead trees. The quetzal is a fruit-eating bird. One of its preferred snacks is the wild avocado, which it swallows whole. After digestion, it regurgitates the seed, often long distances away. Some scientists believe that wild avocados are somewhat dependent on quetzals for seed dispersal. Quetzals are regionally migratory, making conservation of its habitat challenging in a relatively small country of over 13 million people and dwindling forestlands.

Ancient Mayans and Aztecs worshipped Quetzalcoatl, the Plumed Serpent, as a god. He usually is depicted wearing an elaborate headdress of quetzal feathers. So revered was Quetzalcoatl that the Mayans made killing the bird a crime punishable by death! The Aztecs and Mayans perfected the art of trapping quetzals, removing the prized tail plumage, then releasing them to grow new feathers.

Today, they still are esteemed by the descendents of the Mayans and are the national symbol of Guatemala. The country's currency is the quetzal, and both coins and paper denominations portray the bird in profile, in order to show off its magnificent tail. Travelers to the cloud forests in the Chuchumantanes Mountains often are frustrated in their attempts to add the quetzal to their identification lists. They are reclusive birds, and deforestation has destroyed much of the mountain forest habitat in which they thrive. For those unable to track one in the wild, the Guatemalan natural history museum in the capital has a stuffed quetzal proudly displayed.

In a country with a long history of conflict between descendents of the native Mayans and the Europeans who came to dominate them, the quetzal might be seen as a cause of hope, a symbol both of the Mayan past and the modern future of the country.

This is the Acropolis at the National Park of Tikal of Petén, Guatemala. Tikal has become the most famous of the "lost cities" of the Mayans. Although dozens of other Mayan cities have been excavated, Tikal is the symbol of Mayan culture that eventually included not only Guatemala but also the western portions of Honduras and El Salvador, all of the Yucatán Peninsula, and parts of present-day Mexico.

3

Guatemala Through Time

S een from the air, the ancient Mayan city of Tikal rises out of the thick rain forest like a giant Lego model, its sun-bleached stones pointing skyward. Since 1956, when archeologists began uncovering Tikal's mysterious past, it has become the most famous of the "lost cities" of the Mayans. Although dozens of other ancient ceremonial cities have been uncovered and excavated in Guatemala, Tikal is the symbol of Mayan achievement. The city's white stones, which gleam against the surrounding emerald forest, reflect the mysterious contradictions of its builders.

In the region that is now Guatemala, one of the most highly developed and stable cultures in the Western Hemisphere thrived for centuries before the coming of European explorers. The Mayan culture eventually spread to include not only present-day Guatemala and the western portions of Honduras and El Salvador but all of the

Yucatán Peninsula and the present-day Mexican states of Tabasco and Chiapas.

This ancient civilization accomplished remarkable feats of engineering and science. Today, we remember them principally as the master builders of Tikal and other elaborate cities. Some of these urban areas were home to more than 30,000 people, making them among the largest cities in the ancient world. The Mayans also were among the world's most expert astronomers and mathematicians. Their calendar was more accurate than that used by the sixteenth-century Spanish conquerors. Their system of mathematics included the concept of the zero long before Europeans adopted it from an ancient Eastern source. Yet these brilliant architects and astronomers never used the wheel as a tool, considering it a child's toy. Having no beasts of burden, they carried goods on their backs, as their descendents do today.

Based largely on architectural evidence, archeologists have described a cultural timeline for the Mayans. It begins with the first distinctively Mayan buildings in the second century B.C. and ends with the last dated inscription on a building, A.D. 908. After this, the Mayan region was invaded and dominated by other groups from the central Mexican plateau—the Toltecs and, somewhat later, the Aztecs. Because of the subregional differences of styles and the slow diffusion of decorative elements throughout the Yucatán region and beyond, some overlap between periods is indicated.

MAYAN TIMELINE

150 B.C. to A.D. 600	Early Classic
550 B.C. to A.D. 850	Mid-Classic
600 B.C. to A.D. 900	Late Classic
A.D. 900 to 1200	Early Post-Classic (Maya-Toltec Period)

During the classic period, the Mayans built the familiar structures known as pyramids. But Mesoamerican (the term archaeologists use in reference to Middle America) pyramids were different in form and function than those of Egypt. The Mayans built *ziggurats*—flat-topped pyramids. The summits of these structures were designed as stages for rites and rituals, including human sacrifice. Ziggurats were located in ceremonial city centers and typically were surrounded by temples and elaborate ball courts. The most significant structures were connected by walkways of crushed limestone, a building material that the Mayans had in abundance. Evidently these cities contained many wooden structures as well. Traces of them have vanished, however, due to centuries of exposure to tropical heat and humidity.

Using a mortar made of sand and lime, the ancient builders created durable broad-based stone terraces for their pyramids, some of which reached heights of more than 200 feet above the forest floor. Ornamental walls on the flat tops, called roof combs, added to the imposing height. Temples and pyramids were adorned with intricate sculpture and carving. Inscriptions indicating the lineage of city rulers and the dates of special events were carved on the lintels above doorways. Depictions of ceremonies and ceremonial masks were carved on wall panels. Other decorative designs blended human figures with serpents, jaguars, and plants. Temple entrances were decorated with fantastic animal features, making the doorways look like enormous fanged mouths. In the same way that human and animal figures were merged for decorative and religious purposes, Mayan building design blended natural forms with architectural elements. For instance, stone columns were carved to resemble trees.

Although the Mayans were master builders, they did not create any regional transportation network linking their great cities. In a region that stretched from the northern Yucatán Peninsula south to the rugged highlands and into Honduras and El Salvador, this lack of connection encouraged self-sufficiency among local rulers. Over time, Tikal, and other major urban areas such as Palenque and Quirigua, became almost entirely independent. Much as the ancient Greek culture was distributed among autonomous city-states, the Mayan culture consisted of people who were widely separated and politically independent. Over the centuries of the classic Mayan era, regional differences in building style, urban patterns, and political leadership developed. The major architectural and cultural subregions were the Motagua Valley, Usumacinta Valley, the Highlands, and the Eastern Coast.

RELIGION

The term "sacral society" is sometimes applied to contemporary Mayan villages in Guatemala. A sacral society is one in which religion, politics, economics, and social life in general are tightly interwoven. Ancient Mayan society was also sacral, at least in the urban areas in and around the ceremonial cities.

Although they shared essential cultural practices, the ancient Mayans were not a unified group. Rather, they were a collection of different national groups that shared basic fundamental traits. Religion is an example of a cultural attribute that united the Mayans under a set of general belief systems and practices. Yet all of the Mayan tribes did not share even that. Each city-state and its surrounding peoples developed its own variation of faith out of a general background of belief common to all Mayans. Complicating the cultural picture even further is the fact that Mayans and other Mexican and Central American cultures influenced one another greatly over a period of many centuries. Tremendous cultural cross-fertilization occurred among the Olmecs, Mayans, Toltecs, Aztecs, and other groups. Many archaeologists now believe that all these groups had a common origin out of which locally distinctive cultures evolved, much like variations on a theme.

A Mayan priest offers incense and lights candles on a ceremonial pyre in the sacred city of Iximche on the jurisdiction of Chimaltenango, which lies 60 miles (90 kilometers) west of Guatemala City. On June 4, 1999, Mayans in Guatemala gathered for the first time to publicly celebrate the Day of the Eight Sacred Threads, calling for unity of the indigenous populations of Guatemala.

In the Mayan version of the religious beliefs common to Central America and Mexico, an important distinction was made between ancient gods and younger gods. In the Mayan belief system, the older gods were associated with natural forces of weather, animals, plants, and the control of agriculture. In sharp contrast, the younger gods were intimately involved in the affairs of humans. They controlled or influenced the behavior of infants and children, magic spells and incantations, and aspects of daily life. The Mayans adopted these younger deities from the Toltecs. Quetzalcoatl, the Plumed Serpent, was considered the greatest of the Toltec gods, and the Mayans came to embrace him as their central deity as well.

Much of what we know today about sacral Mayan culture comes from the *Popol Vuh*, the sacred text of the Quiche Maya. This text contains the history and many beliefs of the Quiche people, one of the major linguistic subgroups in the region of Mayan culture. The *Popol Vuh* was compiled in Latin from oral traditions of the Quiche by an unknown, but obviously highly educated, Mayan scribe in about 1550. A parish priest in the highland village of Chichicastenango copied this original manuscript in the language of the Quiche at the end of the seventeenth century. The original was lost soon after. Some historians speculate that other copies of the *Popol Vuh* may still exist, hidden away from the prying eyes of outsiders by the descendents of the Quiche Maya.

According to the creation myth in this holy text, humans were shaped out of maize after a battle between the elder gods of creation and the lords of the underworld. In twenty-first century Guatemala, the elder nature gods—the gods of the sun, rain, and maize—are still worshipped, mostly in the form of Christian saints. The first humans created by these gods— four men and four women—were the beginnings of the three major Quiche tribes. Each tribe was subdivided further into fourfold and threefold family and social arrangements as well. As we will see, numerology was an important ordering device for the Mayans. More than any other ancient Central American people, Mayans set a supreme religious value on time and units of time as defining structures for life and as objects of worship.

The arrangement and measuring of time were central to the Mayan view of the universe. Priests jealously guarded the secrets of a complex numerological system. One of the basic measures of reckoning in this system was a ritual time unit of 260 days called a *tzolkin*. The priests considered tzolkins as 260 different combinations of the gods that influenced numbers (13 gods) and days (20 gods). Another powerful unit of time was the Mayan solar year, or *haab*, which consisted of 365 days. The combination of the haab and tzolkin resulted in elaborately constructed number sets that no one other than the priests understood. The most important of these sets, a *katun*, measured a period of 7,200 days. An elaborate theory of determinism was based on the katuns, which evidently described cycles in the development of Mayan culture and were believed to give priests their powers of prediction.

Just as the Western calendar we use today starts at year "0" (the birth of Christ) and moves forward from that point, so the Mayan calendar begins with a year "0." The Mayan year 0 corresponds to the year 3113 B.C. in our Julian calendar.

The priests were continually correcting their calendar, and eventually they made it the most accurate ever developed. The Mayan calendar ends abruptly in the year A.D. 2012, although no explanation has been found indicating what happens after that point in time. Just as the origins of Mayan astronomy and mathematics are mysterious, so, too, is the "end of time" in their calendar.

Numbers also were basic to the Mayan understanding of the ordering of the cosmos. This cosmology was based on an elaborate system of four horizontal and three vertical directions. Color also was an important aspect of cosmic order. For the Mayans, red was the color of the east, yellow was associated with the south, black was west, and north was white. Mayan cosmology combined Earth space (the four cardinal directions and their colors), cosmic space (the three vertical directions), and human duality (men and women). Direction, color, time, and cosmic forces were all connected in a dense web of personal fate and preordained events. Mayan priests believed they could predict and somewhat shape events in the future by manipulating combinations of these forces.

The complex spiritual world of the Mayans included a system of magic grounded in the belief that each person had an animal counterpart who shared that person's fate. Since an animal shared a person's fate, one could harm an enemy or rival by identifying and harming his counterpart in the animal world. Elaborate spells and rituals evolved from this belief, and magic incantations for protection from spells were a part of daily life.

MAYAN SOCIAL CLASSES

Mayan society was divided into rigidly defined groups with strict social and political lines separating them. The term for this social categorization is stratification. Depending on their status in the social hierarchy, people in a rigidly stratified society have very different lifestyles. Inequality is a main feature of stratification, and Mayan society manifested vastly unequal classes.

Classic Mayans were born into one of three main social groups. The most powerful consisted of priests and warriors. Priests ruled over the Mayan political system since they were thought to be the source of predictions about the future, with the proper means to appease the various deities. As protectors of the temples, warriors benefited from a high status as well, enjoying pampered lives in the ceremonial cities.

The second class included merchants and artisans. Members of the artisan class were valued for the skills and techniques they developed in ornamenting the temples and other public buildings. The more talented an artist was, the more likely it was that he had a powerful priest or warrior as a patron and protector. Merchants composed the economic class of the society. Ancient Mayans were shrewd traders, exchanging crafts and jewelry with people from thousands of miles away. Today, a visitor to a Mayan village on market day can see the merchant spirit alive and well. Haggling, bartering, and trading are constant activities. On the hierarchy's bottom rung were the workers—farmers and armies of stone workers—who supplied the vast labor needed in constructing the ceremonial cities and in raising crops to feed the urban populations.

Just as they created beautiful forms and motifs for their buildings, Mayans decorated their bodies in fantastic ways as well. Whether a child was born into the elite priestly or warrior class, or into the lowest rungs of society, it was subjected to deformation. At the age of only a few days, infants were tied onto a device consisting of two hinged boards. The wedge created by the boards put pressure on the infant's malleable skull and eventually produced a flattened, sloping forehead. For reasons no one can explain, crossed eyes also were considered desirable. Parents hung small objects directly between a newborn's eyes, causing an inward rotation and, eventually, a cross-eyed child. Elaborate facial and body tattoos were stylish among the elite, and women of all classes filed their teeth to razor sharp points. The faces that resulted from these techniques can be seen portrayed in the carvings and wall frescoes that have survived the centuries deep in the temples and terraced pyramids.

DECLINE OF CLASSIC MAYAN CULTURE

For reasons that remain shrouded in mystery, new Mayan temple and city construction stopped abruptly. At about the same time, established administrative and religious centers were abandoned. The production of stonework, jade carvings, and pottery also ceased. Scientists do not agree on what caused this rapid decline in classic Mayan culture, but we do know it happened between A.D. 908 and 915.

Some researchers believe an environmental disaster overcame the Mayans. Scientists point to evidence of increased sedimentation in Mayan lakes during the period of abrupt cultural decline and disintegration. Lake and river sedimentation—the depositing of sediment or soil in the water—is a problem anywhere slash-and-burn shifting cultivation is practiced. This style of agriculture was common throughout the Yucatán and supported the populations of the Mayan cities. Perhaps extensive slash-and-burn practices resulted in widespread soil exhaustion and the erosion of fragile tropical soils.

In a region where natural disasters such as earthquakes,

volcanic eruptions, and hurricanes are common, a combination of disastrous storms and quakes may have demoralized Mayan populations already stressed by failing crops. Perhaps a collapse of the agricultural system weakened the power of the priests, who now were seen to be fallible. This, in turn, may have led to social upheavals. The labor class, which outnumbered the elites, may have risen in revolt against the tyranny of the priests. Perhaps warfare between the city-states destroyed the power of the elites. Theories of the collapse abound.

Archeologists estimate that perhaps as many lost Mayan cities wait to be discovered as have been found. Hidden in remote, sparsely populated areas, these ruins tantalize archaeologists and other scientists who have worked for over a hundred years to understand what brought about the collapse of classic Mayan civilization. Perhaps the answer is waiting to be unearthed in one of the still-lost ancient cities.

Whatever the cause, the city-states came under the military control of the Toltecs and, later, the Aztecs. Both groups were warlike tribes from the highlands of central Mexico. Each had adopted many cultural features of the Mayans, who now, in turn, were heavily influenced by the invading northerners. Approximately two centuries after the Aztecs extended their domain south to include most of Mesoamerica, the first Europeans entered the region. The traditional way of life was changed forever, and a new cultural exchange began that worked to the advantage of the technologically and politically more highly developed Europeans.

THE EUROPEANS

On his fourth and final voyage to the New World, Christopher Columbus sailed along the eastern coast of Central America. He was searching for a passage through the American landmass that would allow him to sail on to the riches of eastern Asia. Columbus, of course, never found this passage because it does not exist. But in the account of the voyage written by his son,

Archaeologists believe that many lost Mayan cities wait to be discovered or rediscovered. Upon further excavation of this Mayan royal palace in Cancuen in the Peten rain forest, archaeologists became convinced that it was one of the largest, most elaborate, and best preserved of the ancient Mayan palaces. The structure is three stories high with 170 rooms built around 11 courtyards and dates back to the eighth century.

Fernando, there is a reference to what might have been the first meeting between Europeans and Mayans. Somewhere just off the coast of Guatemala and Honduras, Columbus took several people on board from a light canoe. One of them supplied the explorer with information about the region and the coastline to the southeast. Columbus later released these native Amerindians (the preferred term for American Indians), and they fade from Fernando's narrative. But circumstantial evidence points to these as having been Mayans of the Post-Classical period.

The Spanish, who quickly followed Columbus to Central America, were focused on riches rather than exploration. The conquistadors were looking for "El Dorado," the fabled City of Gold. The promise of quick riches lured them first into the interior of Mexico and then south into Guatemala. In 1522, less than twenty years after Columbus's last voyage, Cortéz conquered Mexico and founded Mexico City on the ruins of the Aztec empire.

In 1524, one of Cortéz's lieutenants, Pedro de Alvarado, was sent south to conquer the Mayans and search Guatemala for plunder. With only 300 men, Alvarado crushed the highland Mayans and founded the Spanish settlement that became Guatemala City. His military campaign is one of the cruelest chapters in the Spanish conquest of New World people.

Mayans were short in stature compared to average Europeans of the sixteenth century, which gave the Spanish a psychological edge over the natives, both during and after the conquest. This advantage was compounded by the Spanish use of horses, which made the mounted conquistadors appear huge and powerful. The horses must have been terrifying aspects of Alvarado's campaign. At least initially, native people through-out the region believed that the figures they encountered in battle were four-footed giants, half man and half fantastic creature. Of more long-term importance to the conquest was the fact that the Spaniards possessed superior weaponry, including effective body armor.

Fighting between the Spanish and the Mayans continued sporadically throughout the sixteenth and seventeenth centuries. As you will see in Chapter 4, the old conflict between European and Mayan cultures continues into our own time.

A few years after Alvarado's conquest, Mexico City was established as the capital of the Viceroyalty of New Spain. Guatemala City became the second city of the Viceroyalty, a regional administrative center for the lands that stretched south to Costa Rica. Through the seventeenth and eighteenth centuries, the country was relegated to the backwaters of Spain's New World Empire. It lacked the gold and silver of Peru and Mexico, and its Mayan inhabitants resisted Spanish culture. Spain invested little and received little in return from its Guatemala colony.

INDEPENDENCE

Centuries of imperial neglect came to a close in 1821 when Spain's loose grip on Mesoamerica was relinquished. Independence came not only to Guatemala, but also to the other Spanish colonies of the region—Mexico, Honduras, El Salvador, Nicaragua, and Costa Rica. Like Guatemala, these other colonies had languished under Spain's long rule. With a common colonial history, a common colonial language, and similar political economies, the six countries established the Central American Federation (CAF) in 1823. The CAF was a bold experiment that failed quickly. The lack of any inter-regional transportation system made it difficult to communicate over the rugged mountains and dense forests of the vast territory of the federation, which stretched from the Rio Grande in the north to the Gulf of Darien in the south, more than 2,000 miles. A lack of common goals and concerns led to the peaceful dissolution of the federation, which formally ended in 1838. Local economic and political elites filled the political vacuum by organizing independent republics along the territorial lines of the old colonies.

Guatemala's Spanish colonial administration had not prepared the country for independence. Industrialization, which had begun in North America in the early nineteenth century, did not come to Central America until much later. The national economy was based on Spanish landowners who cultivated sugar cane and other crops on relatively small land holdings. They also raised cochineal, the traditional red dye of Mesoamerica that is extracted from insects. A few very small cattle operations were established in the far eastern portion of the country. Most of the Mayan population continued to live off the land, practicing subsistence agriculture much as their ancestors had done.

Searching for a means to develop the agricultural export economy, landowners watched the rapid rise of coffee as an export crop in Costa Rica. In the late 1830s, they began importing the techniques and tools necessary to compete with their former partners in the CFA for a share in the growing coffee market. Starting on farms and ranches already growing the prickly pear cacti upon which the cochineal lived, coffee production began modestly in 1840 and spread slowly.

Guatemala did not begin exporting coffee beans until 1873, almost 40 years after Costa Rica's first bags were shipped to Colombia, then on to Europe. Although Guatemala took much longer than Costa Rica to develop a coffee export industry, it quickly caught up with Costa Rica in production. By the mid-1880s, it was the largest producer of the four coffee countries of Central America: Costa Rica, El Salvador, Nicaragua, and Guatemala. Guatemalan success in developing coffee into a cash crop led to the spread of coffee agriculture to neighboring Honduras in 1912.

One of the reasons coffee exports lagged behind those of Costa Rica for so long was the lack of a national transportation system, a problem that persists into the twenty-first century in some parts of Guatemala. Early coffee growers had no means of moving their beans to port other than a crude and often muddy ox cart road built in the 1850s for the cochineal trade. It was not until 1912 that rail lines linked the most important coffee districts with ocean ports.

Slow economic development masked the old animosities between Europeans and Mayans. Before entering the world agricultural market with coffee and then later with bananas, Guatemala was a land in which Mayans and the descendents of the Spanish settlers lived in separate worlds. With an increase in demand for agriculturally productive land in the late nineteenth century, these worlds collided. The clash between Indian communalism and the private property system of the Europeans has characterized Guatemalan politics ever since.

Beginning in the 1860s, Indian land rights were commonly violated by European coffee growers. Landowners often rented communally held Indian land, grew coffee for a few years, and then sold the land to other Europeans as though it were their own. This practice became so widespread that many Indian villages refused to rent land to coffee growers. This resistance came at a time when Guatemala's coffee exports were expanding, and the demand for new lands was great. In 1877, a national law privatized large portions of communal land that growers wanted to bring into production. This set a precedent for successive Guatemalan governments that consistently have backed the demands of coffee growers and other European interests at the expense of traditional Indian land rights.

In the ancient culture hearth of the Mayas, the oldest political and economic conflicts in the Western Hemisphere are still simmering. In fact, many of Guatemala's social and political problems have their roots in this age-old dispute over land between Europeans and Mayans. Now that the country has come to an uneasy peace with itself, there is reason to hope that these ancient conflicts may be settled eventually.

This Cakchiquel woman lives in a village in the western highlands called San Antonio Aguas Calientes. She is making tortillas, which are a part of a typical meal in Guatemala.

CHAPTER 4

People and Culture

San Antonio Aguas Calientes, a village in the western highlands, is a settlement of about 600 people. Located in an upland basin in the tierra templada, San Antonio is generally typical of Mayan life in the country's rural areas. Most of the residents are Cakchiquel, one of Guatemala's major linguistic and tribal groups.

Except for the main road, all of the streets are unpaved. Footpaths winding into San Antonio are often lined with chichicasta plants, a stinging nettle used to discourage trespassing. Here a visitor gets the sense of an ancient way of life little changed for centuries. From a cultural perspective, this is true. Many highland Mayans carry on life as their ancestors did a thousand years ago.

Children are a constant presence in the mountain villages, as they are elsewhere in the country. Guatemala has one of the highest total fertility rates (TFR) in the Western Hemisphere, about 4.5. A common

47

demographic measure, the TFR is the average number of children a woman will have in her lifetime. (For comparison, the TFR in the United States is about 2.1.) High fertility rates indicate much about a country's culture and economy. For one thing, a high rate usually means that a country has a very low doubling time. This is the time it will take for a population to double in size (at current rates of growth). With a doubling time of about 20 years, Guatemala faces increased demands for education, employment, and land. All are in short supply. At the current rate of population growth, by the year 2023, this country of crowded cities, dwindling farmlands, and disappearing rain forests will have to contend with 26 million people.

Because of their high rates of population growth, less developed countries face severe political and economic problems. Nevertheless, people in these agricultural societies have good reasons for having lots of children. In countries lacking any social safety net, children represent old age security for their parents. And where subsistence labor is in demand, children have high economic value. Another factor is that in less-developed regions, infant and child mortality is high. Parents have more children in these countries because children still represent a basic means of survival. But high TFRs usually indicate problems in the areas of health, nutrition, and educational attainment. Here, too, the numbers on Guatemala are sobering. The infant mortality rate is 79 per 1,000, and the maternal mortality is 110 per 1,000. These figures make Guatemala one of the worst places in the Western Hemisphere for infant, child, and maternal well being. According to UN nutrition surveys, approximately 50 percent of the country's children are malnourished. Education spending is the lowest in the Western Hemisphere, next to Haiti.

The World Bank reports that Guatemala has the third-highest degree of income inequality in the world among low and middle-income countries. This means that relatively few people hold a disproportionate amount of the national wealth and that most people struggle hard just to survive.

Behind the statistics, however, lies the reality of a life that is sometimes violent but also fraught with meaning and the comforts of cultural continuity. Looking at daily life among the Mayans of the Sierra Madre gives a sense of this reality better than numbers and percentages do. Examining cultural identity and the ways in which it is expressed is a good place to begin this profile of life in the mountains.

TRAJE, WEAVING, AND CULTURAL IDENTITY

Traje is the name for traditional Mayan costumes, worn primarily by women and girls but also by men in some remote areas. Throughout the long civil war (1960–1996), the army targeted men wearing traje as guerrilla sympathizers. For purposes of survival, many males abandoned traje in favor of the national dress of Guatemalan workers. This generic clothing consists of jeans, boots, and cowboy shirt, topped off with a big white cowboy hat. Seeing groups of Guatemalan men or boys all wearing virtually identical outfits, a visitor might think that there was a national uniform.

Next to the conventionally dressed and predictably drab men, Mayan women appear as beautiful tropical birds. This is, after all, the "land where the rainbow begins." Popular culture commentators have suggested that the inspiration for the brightly colored dress of the "hippies" in the United States during the sixties was the highland traje. Young U.S. travelers brought back the richly colored and fancifully decorated dress of the highlands and made it a standard for psychedelic costumes.

The basis for female traje is a colorful embroidered blouse, called a *huipil*. Huipils are handmade for family members as daily dress, although the initial reaction to traje by outsiders is to think that these are special "dress up" outfits. Part of the appeal of the huipil is that it is meant to be worn and to be seen as part of daily life. Collectors and museum curators "discovered" traje years ago, and so, today, one may find huipiles in art galleries, museums, and exhibitions around the world. Traders from

While some men work in the clothing and textile trade, it is the women who keep the tradition of weaving alive. This family of weavers carrying their wares in the village of Panajachel are on their way to market.

the United States and Europe travel regularly to Guatemala specifically to purchase traje and bring it home, where it fetches a big price. A handmade huipil might sell for $40 in a mountain market town and end up in a Los Angeles boutique with a $300 price tag!

The bottom half of the traje is called a *corte*, a skirt fashioned from a long length of cloth that contains identifying colors and symbols. Another element of traje is the *cinta*, an elaborate cloth hair adornment. Although not formally a part of traje, the *tzute* is worn almost daily by women as they perform their tasks. The tzute is an all-purpose carryall for tortillas, firewood, or babies.

While some men work in the clothing and textile trade, it is Mayan women who keep the ancient arts alive. Traje is worn primarily by Mayan women and produced almost exclusively by them as well. Significantly, it is the women who make clothing worn by the family. Already abandoned by most men, traje, however, is disappearing slowly among young women, especially if they migrate to Guatemala City, where they usually will adopt Western dress.

Mayan traditionalists continue one of the oldest continuously practiced weaving techniques in the world. Mayan women were weaving by 1500 B.C. and, as the holy book of the Quiche Maya commands them, they have not forgotten the old ways. This sacred book, the *Popol Vuh*, contains the following command, taken seriously by many Guatemalans: "Children, wherever you may be, do not abandon the crafts taught to you . . . because they are the crafts passed down to you by our forebearers. If you forget them, you will betray your lineage."

Rigoberta Menchu is a contemporary Quiche Mayan who is known as a Nobel Peace Prize winner and human rights activist. Although she has spent much of her adult life in exile in the United States, Europe, and Mexico, she continues to wear traje, explaining her choice this way: "We express ourselves through our designs, through our dress—our huipil, for instance, is like an image of our ancestors."

Although traditional clothing styles and forms are sometimes machine made, most traje is still created on the basic tool of traditional weavers, the backstrap loom. It is a simple device consisting of two bars; one is tied to a support, and the other goes around the weaver's waist. The weaver controls tension in the loom by leaning back or forward. The backstrap looms seen in the highlands today are almost identical in form to those used for a thousand years. With the daily work required of Mayan women, the loom had to be easy to pack up and move. As a result, it is light and portable and one can see women weaving outdoors, their looms tied to trees, as they watch their children or keep birds out of their gardens.

Weaving on a backstrap loom is very time consuming. An ordinary huipil can take three months to complete, while an elaborately designed ceremonial one might take twice as long. Whatever the final style, the result of careful work with a backstrap loom is high-quality cloth prized by Mayans and increasingly sought after by collectors worldwide. To non-Mayans, the brilliant combinations of rich color and stylistic designs of the huipil might seem quaint. To Mayans, however, the colors and symbols tell a story of identity.

Each huipil contains a coded message to those who can read it. The patterns, colors, and figures displayed on a huipil indicate a woman's home village and her linguistic affiliation. In a land of almost two dozen major Mayan tongues, a traditional highland person can glance at a huipil and instantly know the wearer's language and home region. A woman's marital standing—single, married, widowed—is coded into the huipil as well. Among the community of weavers themselves, an artfully woven huipil also reveals the creator's status as a weaver and artist. In Mayan Guatemala, you are who your clothes say you are.

Within the hieroglyphic-like language of the huipil, traditional designs utilize figures with specific religious and cultural references. Some of these are nearly universal figures among Mayan tribes. The sacred ceiba tree, the yaxche, turns up again and again throughout the highlands, regardless of village or tribe. The backward-glancing coyote, which brought maize to man in the early days of creation, is another common figure.

The backstrap loom seen in the highlands today is almost identical in form to those in use for a thousand years. It is light and portable and, as this woman demonstrates, can be used outdoors on the street in Antigua.

The feathered serpent, Quetzalcoatl, perhaps the most powerful of all the old gods, turns up repeatedly. Zigzags indicate the god of lightning as well as the ritual walkways up the steep sides of the ziggurats. Other elements are of more recent vintage. Horses and peacocks, for example, were unknown to the ancients. Brought to Central America by the Spanish in the sixteenth century, these animals caught the fancy of the weavers, who came to associate these figures with Spanish culture.

Along with clothing and the values associated with traditional weaving, cultural identity for Mayans is complicated by the fact that the Mayan language is fragmented into dozens of tongues. Over 50 languages are spoken in Guatemala. Some of these languages are kept alive by only a few thousand speakers in remote areas of the country. Spanish is a common second tongue for most people, although many Mayans are not fluent Spanish speakers. Most of the Europeanized ladinos speak only Spanish. Some language groups are quite large. Just as in other Amerindian regions of the Western Hemisphere, the name of the language is commonly used to identify the tribal group as well.

MAJOR MAYAN LINGUISTIC AND TRIBAL GROUPS

Cakchiquel (380,000 speakers, six major regional dialects)

Mam (450,000 speakers, five dialects)

Quiche (600,000 speakers, six dialects)

Tzutujil (82,000 speakers, two dialects)

Kekchi (400,000 speakers, three dialects)

Pokomchi (90,000 speakers, two dialects)

RELIGION

Another important marker of cultural identity is religion. The predominant faith in Guatemala is Roman Catholicism. Among the 55 percent of Guatemala's 13 million people who are Mayan, syncretism is widely practiced. Syncretism is a term for the blending or merging of different religious or philosophical belief systems. Syncretic religious practices take varying forms, depending on the beliefs being combined. No one has a firm estimate for the number of Mayans who combine Catholicism with traditional religion, but the number must be high. Travel to any highland village and you can find evidence of syncretism in the people's daily life.

The market village of Chichicastenango, for example, is a place where visitors can watch syncretism in action. On designated market days, members of *cofradias* (religious brotherhoods) take up central positions on the steep steps of the Catholic Church. Here they tend small ceremonial

Mayans hoist a giant paper kite before flying it over a cemetery outside Guatemala City. Such kites take weeks to make and are flown over grave-yards in an annual competition in the weeks following the Catholic feasts of All Saints and All Souls on November 2. Mayans believe the kites allow them to communicate with the souls of their departed loved ones.

fires and for a small fee will perform a brief prayer, asking the saints within the church and the old gods, presumably without, for help. Armed usually with nothing more than a bottle of cheap locally made rum for splashing on the fire, the cofradia embody the syncretic life of the highlands.

Devout Catholics, cofradia members also visit caves in the volcanic mountains around Lake Atitlán where they guide the faithful to spots where Mayan deities are believed to reside. In these sacred caves, gifts to the gods pile up—flowers, bundles of incense, hardboiled eggs, small pieces of cloth, bottles of rum or fruit juice.

Chichicastenango is a traditional highland village that is famous for its twice-a-week market. These hand-carved masks can be found on display there.

Another common example of syncretic belief is found around the numerous ancient Mayan carvings that picket the mountains. In places where these are easily accessed on foot, people visit regularly, leaving offerings of food or flowers. The soot and ashes of ceremonial fires usually ring these sites.

DAILY LIFE IN THE HIGHLANDS

A strict gender division defines Mayan life. Men work the fields. Women weave, raise children, cook, and tend small gardens. Children attend public school through the sixth grade. After that, they probably will become agricultural workers like their fathers or weavers like their mothers. Relatively few highland Mayans make it to high school.

Gathering firewood for cooking and heating is a task usually performed by children. In a growing country where deforestation is a serious problem, finding wood for fuel can take up hours of labor a week for a small family.

Houses are made of bamboo and wood and are commonly called "stick houses." Roofs are fashioned from tin or metal. The kitchen is usually in a separate structure from the sleeping area. Cooking is done on a concrete platform with a deep center recess where fires are built. A typical meal consists of some combination of tortillas, beans, corn, peppers, and eggs. Meat dishes, such as spicy chicken stew, are for special occasions. Minimum wage law does not cover the kinds of seasonal day labor that are available in the highlands, where the average wage is about $6 a day, so extravagant food purchases are rare. Most families maintain small garden plots to supplement their diets.

In a country famous for its specialty coffee—a one-pound bag of which sells for $8-12 in the United States—most Mayans drink the dregs, literally, of the coffee harvest. They say they can't afford to drink the best of the crop that they themselves harvest.

Market towns and market days are significant cultural features of daily Mayan life. Traditional Mayan villages were specialized in agricultural production as well as in weaving and handcrafts. The market system developed as a means to exchange necessary items. On market days, held on different days of the week in different villages, people come from as far away as ten miles, usually on foot, to barter, trade, sell, buy, and socialize. Everything from fresh fruit and vegetables, live chickens, traditional weavings and handcrafts, to factory-made toys and tools can be found.

Negotiating a price—haggling—is a standard part of market day shopping. Sellers expect buyers to challenge their prices, and the art of haggling is held in high regard. Experienced Mayan traders view buyers who don't engage in haggling as being naive, at best. The traditional type of economic exchange known as bartering also takes place at the markets. Chichicastenango is a traditional highland village famous for its twice-a-week market. Smaller villages have one market day a week.

The market at Solola is held twice a week. Everything from fresh fruit and vegetables, live chickens, and traditional weavings to factory-made toys and tools can be found here.

A cultural bridge between Mayan village life and westernized urban culture is music. The national instrument of Guatemala is the marimba, a member of the xylophone family of mallet instruments. Marimba music is to Guatemala what reggae is to Jamaica, or mariachi is to Mexico—an omnipresent sound enjoyed by natives (both Mayan and ladino) and visitors alike. Musicologists are uncertain of the marimba's Central American origins. Many believe it came to the New World in the sixteenth century with West Coast African slaves. However it came, it is now found everywhere, from orchestra settings in Guate (Guatemala City) to the smallest mountain village fiesta. It may appear suddenly on the street, carried by five or six musicians who stand like musical sentinels in a row behind the wooden keys. They pound out an exotic tune, pass the hat quickly, then hoist the instrument up and disappear down the street. The term "battle of the bands" in towns such as Antigua means a marimba battle. Two groups take up positions on either side of the central town square and trade off melodies. Ladinos swirl in graceful waltz time, and foreign visitors improvise to the music. Off to the side, Mayan listeners stand mute and motionless, seeming to absorb the music as much with their eyes as with their ears.

Traditional Mayan instruments also may be heard, although not as frequently or with as much fanfare. The *tun*, a small drum hung over the shoulder or held between the legs, is the rhythmic accompaniment for the *tzicolaj*, a small wooden flute. The plaintive melodies of the flute are in sharp contrast to the lively marimba, giving the listener an eerie sense of ancient sounds.

More than half of Guatemala's rural population is found in the densely inhabited upland basins and plateaus of the central highlands. Here, and in the Cuchumatanes Mountains to the north, the Mayans maintain their traditional identities. Ladinos, the country's other significant cultural group, usually live apart from Mayan village communities. These are Westernized people of mixed Mayan and Spanish ancestry who tend to live in or near the major urban areas of Guatemala City and Quetzaltenango. Ladinos make up approximately 45 percent of the national population.

LADINOS AND URBAN LIFE

Identity in Guatemala is to a large degree a matter of dress and language, and the ladinos hold themselves apart socially and culturally from Mayans in both these aspects. Their clothing would not be out of place in any North American city. Culturally, ladinos are much like their counterparts in Western popular cultures. They are overwhelmingly urban in their residence and primarily Spanish speaking. To be urban in Guatemala means one thing: to be a resident of Guatemala City, or "Guate," as its residents fondly refer to it.

With a population of 3.5 million people, Guatemala City is

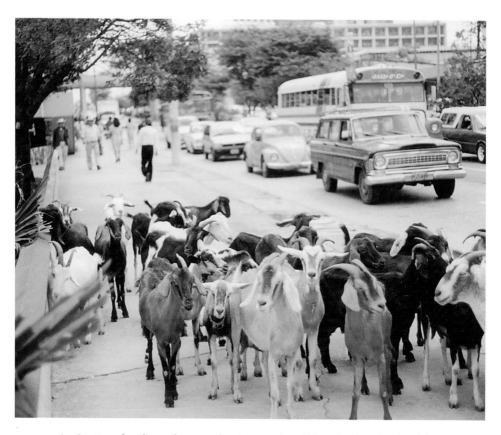

In Guatemala City, urban modernism and traditional culture exist side-by-side. Amidst high-rise office buildings and corporate headquarters, one might see a herd of goats waiting for a traffic light.

the largest urban area in the country. The country's capital, it is also a perfect example of a primate city. "Primate city" is a term applied to large urban areas in developing countries. These cities serve as the center of the country's political and economic decision making. Guate also exemplifies the urban problems of developing countries. Rural migrants swell the city's population. These migrants usually come without jobs, hoping for a better life for themselves and their children. They end up in fast-growing slums on the city outskirts, joining the ranks of the urban unemployed.

In Guatemala City, urban modernism and traditional

cultural values exist side-by-side, making for some interesting encounters. For example, high-rise office buildings, banking and corporate headquarters, government offices, and apartments surround visitors to the city's central business district. City buses and dangerously speeding taxis clog the streets. But suddenly on the sidewalk a flock of menacing-looking goats might block the way! Visiting one of the city's swankiest restaurants in an upscale neighborhood, a visitor might meet a cow out for a stroll, unaccompanied by any human overseer. Even more dramatic is the presence in this bustling city of highland Mayans in traje, slowly making their way through the enormous grid system of streets, seemingly lost in the noise and bustle of the city, on some unknown and perhaps unknowable errand.

On January 14, 2000 Alfonso Portillo took the oath of office as the first elected president since the December 1996 peace agreement ended the 36-year-old civil war.

CHAPTER 5

Government

S tudents of the U.S. political system find Guatemala's government familiar in at least some ways. It is a democratic republic with a modern constitution. Written in 1985, the constitution separates power among three branches: the executive, the legislative, and the judicial. The chief executive, or president, is elected directly in a national election and is limited to one term. The congressional branch is unicameral, unlike the U.S. bicameral organization of House of Representatives and Senate. The Congress elects members of the third branch, the Supreme Court. Individuals are chosen from a list submitted by the bar association, law school deans, and university faculty. There also is a separate Constitutional Court. Although political interference among the congress and the court system by the president has been a problem, Guatemala is strengthening the walls of separation between the three branches steadily. Constitutional reforms passed in

1993 increased the number of judges, reduced the president's term of office, and increased office terms for mayors.

Similar to the United States, Guatemala has two other lower levels of government. The country is subdivided into 22 administrative divisions called departments. Governors appointed by the president administer these subregional branches of the national government. At the local level, popularly elected mayors or councils govern some 330 municipalities.

EARLY POLITICAL DEVELOPMENT

In 1821, Guatemala gained independence from Spain after almost 300 years as a colony. It briefly joined the Mexican Empire, but the inequalities of this arrangement encouraged Guatemalans to break off this one-sided relationship. In 1823, Guatemala joined a federation with five other Central American countries. The United Provinces of Central America, or the Central American Federation as it also was called, lasted only a few years. The members shared little other than a common Spanish colonial history and language. The lack of any transportation or communication links between the countries was another factor leading to its end. The federation was formally dissolved in 1838, although it never had achieved anything other than a paper union between its members.

Although achieving democracy was a popular goal in the 1830s and 1840s, by the mid-nineteenth century a tradition of autocratic rule had become established. For most of the next 130 years, Guatemala experienced coups, military rule, and brutal, oppressive politics.

Land ownership and land rights were the major political problems. Conflict between the Mayans' communal ownership of land and the European system of private property dated back to the earliest years of colonial rule. This conflict became the central irritant of Guatemalan politics after independence and has marred political relations between traditional Mayans and Spanish Guatemalans ever since.

By the end of World War II, Guatemala seemed to be moving in the direction of serious political reform. In 1944, a group of military officers, students, and professionals, called the October Revolutionaries, overthrew the dictatorship of General Jorge Ubico. Open elections were held the next year and a civilian, Juan Jose Arevalo, was elected president.

Arevalo held office until 1951 and began systematic labor and land reforms. Among other achievements considered radical at the time, he abolished the national forced labor laws. These laws required peasants with less than ten acres of land to work 100 days a year, unpaid, on the farms and plantations of large landowners. Arevalo also established a uniform labor code and a social security system, as well as basic education and literacy programs for rural areas. The 1945 constitution that Arevalo supported legalized labor unions, a development that was to lead to major conflicts in the 1950s.

Arevalo's reforms were continued by his democratically elected successor, Jacobo Arbenz, who focused on extending and strengthening the agrarian land reforms. Specifically, Arbenz provided for the expropriation of idle lands on tracts bigger than 223 acres. In other words, large landowners were the targets. The government paid owners current market prices for their expropriated land, and any land under cultivation was exempt from the law. The goal was to do away with the remnants of feudalism that had been transplanted with the original Spanish colonial administration. Nearly half a million peasants received small plots of land. Not everyone was happy with the direction of the changes in government policy, however. More important, Arbenz's progressive politics exceeded what some Guatemalans believed to be reasonable democratic reforms.

CIVIL WAR

Under Arbenz, the Guatemalan Labor Party—a communist group—was granted legal status in 1952. By 1954, communists gained control of Indian and peasant organizations and labor unions, and they held some key government positions. Most Guatemalans supported democracy, but the economic elites of the country considered Arbenz's policies a threat.

Major opposition to the land reforms came from the United States. The United Fruit Company (UFC) had enjoyed tax-exempt exports since 1901. The UFC also held a monopoly on the country's ports and railroad and telegraph system. Called El Pulpo, the Octopus, the UFC was the country's largest landowner, holding over 550,000 acres. Arbenz offered UFC compensation for its idle lands, based on the UFC's own tax records and current land prices. The company refused an offer of $1.2 million and made a counteroffer of $16 million, a sum far beyond the means of the government.

The U.S. Central Intelligence Agency (CIA) began a destabilization campaign to overthrow the government. In 1954, Colonel Carlos Armas invaded Guatemala from Honduras with the backing of the CIA and toppled the democratic government.

The new U.S.-backed government began persecuting Arbenz supporters. The land reforms and rural education and health policies of the previous ten years were rolled back. The non-elected military leaders took increasingly dictatorial measures against the Mayan Indians and agricultural workers. In 1960, dissident army officers staged an uprising to protest the dictatorial and increasingly corrupt government. Two popular army officers became leaders of an insurgent movement in the eastern regions of Izabal and Zacapa. Thus began Guatemala's long national nightmare of civil war and repression.

Over the long conflict, four major guerrilla groups took shape: the Guerrilla Army of the Poor, the Revolutionary Organization of Armed People, the Rebel Armed Forces, and the Guatemalan Labor Party. Initially, these groups had differing ideas about how best to fight the war. Some engaged in economic sabotage. Others targeted government facilities and attacked the army in the countryside. Sometimes, these groups conducted armed attacks in Guatemala City and other urban areas. They assassinated many important figures, including U.S. Ambassador John Gordon Mein in 1968. U.S. sympathy for the plight of civilians who were suffering in the crossfire between guerrillas and the government vanished after Mein was murdered. A few years later, however, awareness in the United States of the ethnic aspects of the civil war and of the terrible cost in civilian lives increased with the 1983 publication of *I, Rigoberta Menchu, An Indian Woman in Guatemala*. The book was widely read, and its author became an internationally known campaigner for Indian rights.

The government developed an effective tactic for fighting the rebels. The Guatemalan army encouraged the formation of local civilian defense patrols (PACs). PAC participation was in theory voluntary, but the reality was that many Guatemalans had no choice but to join either the PACs or the rebels, especially in the central and western highlands where anti-government feelings among the Mayans were widespread.

Without any real backing from outside the country, the rebel groups fought to a stalemate with the government, which was becoming isolated from the international community over the issue of civilian deaths. In 1982, the four guerrilla groups united under one organization, the Organization of Guatemalan National Revolutionary Unity (URNG), for the purpose of negotiating with the government.

Throughout the civil war, extreme right-wing groups and vigilantes, including the Secret Anti-Communist Army (ESA) and the paramilitary White Hand, tortured and murdered anyone suspected of leftist sympathies. The term "death squad" was applied to these vigilantes who usually worked with the full cooperation of the government forces. The term *desaparecido* (the "disappeared") was coined in Guatemala during the 1960s to describe the people—numbering in the tens of thousands— who were kidnapped by these civilian death squads or by government forces and never seen again. Throughout this shameful history, the United States provided military support and training for the increasingly brutal government. International human rights and religious groups, such as Amnesty International and the Catholic Church, publicized the plight of the Guatemalan people during this period, but the United States continued to back the military rulers.

Over the past few years, human rights and Indian rights have become international issues. Two Nobel Peace Prizes have been awarded in recent years to individuals working to improve the rights of Guatemalans. Rigoberta Menchu's Nobel Prize publicized the severe problems of Guatemala's Mayan people, millions of whom are landless and have limited political rights. Oscar Aria, former president of Costa Rica, won the Nobel in 1992 for his Central American Peace Plan, a comprehensive effort to solve the political problems not only of Guatemala, but of El Salvador, Honduras, and Nicaragua as well. These neighboring countries share most of Guatemala's problems, the foremost of which is land rights.

Years of official government repression and discrimination have left a bitter legacy, although steady international pressure and an end to the civil war have created opportunities for new progress in bringing stability and democracy to the country. After the end of the Cold War in the early 1990s, the United States reversed its position of unqualified support for the government. At least three of the four major rebel forces fighting the government called themselves communists. The United States could not address the Guatemalan conflict seriously until after the fall of communism. Now the United States supports the Arias peace plan, as well as other measures aimed at bringing the country prosperity. For example, regional agencies such as the Inter-American Commission on Human Rights of the Organization of American States are working to formalize the rights of indigenous people in a document that could serve as a constitutional element throughout Latin America.

Another issue being addressed has to do with regional security. Guatemala has long claimed the territory of Belize, its

The term *desparecido* ("the disappeared") was coined in Guatemala for those who were kidnapped by civilian death squads or by government forces during the civil war and never seen again. Many of these people ended up in mass graves that have been exhumed in the aftermath of the war. Rigoberta Menchu, who won the Nobel Peace Prize in 1992 for her work to improve the situation of the Mayan people in Guatemala, is shown here at a camp in Rabinal praying with others over a grave where 49 bodies were found.

neighbor to the northeast. Belize, formerly known as British Honduras, became independent in 1981. In the 1970s and 1980s, sniping and armed attacks by the Guatemalan army made the border between the two countries a dangerous place. Conditions gradually improved so that, by 1986, Great Britain and Guatemala reestablished business relations. In 1987, diplomatic relations resumed, and the two countries again began discussing Belize. These negotiations were successful. In 1991, Guatemala recognized Belize as an independent state. The two countries continue to disagree over where the precise boundaries should be drawn, but violence no longer marks the borderlands. Despite this progress, Great Britain still has a small contingent of troops stationed in its former colony, just in case threats of taking Belize by force become reality.

THE PEACE PLAN

Under the guidance of Arias's Central American Peace Plan, the United Nations (UN) sponsored a series of negotiations that bore fruit in 1996. In December of that year, the government of Guatemala and representatives from URNG (the umbrella organization consisting of the four insurgency groups) signed a set of accords ending the 36-year civil war. The major achievements of the agreement generated hope and optimism among long-time observers of Guatemalan politics. The substantive accords included:

- Plans for the resettlement of war refugees (approximately 1 million people) displaced by the army,

- The establishment of a human rights commission,

- Creation of an Indigenous Rights accord that recognizes the rights of Guatemala's Mayan people to live by their own cultural norms,

- Agrarian and land reforms, including environment protection for endangered habitats,

- A one-third reduction in army size and a change in armed forces mission to focus exclusively on external threats.

The 1996 Peace Accords also included an important symbolic element. Basic provisions of the agreement provided for the translation of key documents into several Mayan languages.

Despite this progress, setbacks continue to plague Guatemala's quest for peace. Army officers seeking to avoid prosecution for human rights violations have waged a new round of death squad killings. This revival of Guatemala's infamous death

In December 1996, the Guatemalan peace commission negotiator Richard Aikehed (left) and Guatemalan National Revolutionary Unity commander Jorge Rosal (right) signed a peace treaty that ended 36 years of civil war.

squads targets forensic anthropologists and other investigators working to identify victims of government repression. President Portillo, elected in 1999, stopped implementing the UN-brokered peace accords. Many of Portillo's actions were attempts to roll back reforms. He was criticized for appointing army officers to head the interior ministry and for using troops to fight crime. Paramilitary groups are once again assassinating human rights activists and political opponents.

Efrain Rios Montt, who was the military dictator during the war's worst period, is now a powerful congressman. His party, the Guatemalan Republican Front, has gained power in the legislature, and Montt was elected President of Congress in 1995 and again in 2000. Observers say he encourages the resurgence of violence, in part to cover up his own complicity in past crimes. The Menchu Foundation and other human rights groups have accused Montt of war crimes and crimes against humanity for his policies during the 1980s.

Rios Montt's brief presidency was the bloodiest period of the 36-year civil war. Estimates are that nearly 200,000 mostly unarmed indigenous civilians were killed. Although leftist rebels and right-wing death squads also were responsible for assassinations, disappearances, and torture of noncombatants, the majority of human rights violations were carried out by the Guatemalan military. The awful details of the war are described in the reports of the Historical Clarification Commission (CEH) and the Archbishop's Office for Human Rights (ODHAG). According to CEH estimates, the government was responsible for 93 percent of the deaths that took place. The Archbishop's Office estimated that government forces were responsible for at least 80 percent. Montt himself was overthrown in a military coup in 1983 led by his own Minister of Defense. The minister, who became the next unelected president of the country, justified the coup by saying that corrupt religious fanatics (Montt is a fundamentalist Christian) had taken over the country.

THE TRANSITION TO PEACE

Now that the peace plan is bringing stability to the country, new political parties are emerging to shape the future of Guatemala in the post-war era. International observers considered the 1999 presidential and legislative elections to have been free and fair. Women and Mayan Indians voted in record numbers, although problems remain over the accessibility of polling places in rural areas.

President Portillo's landslide victory was undercut by allegations in 2000 that his party had illegally altered legislation. Following an investigation, the Supreme Court revoked the legislative immunity of those involved, including President of Congress and FRG party leader chief Rios Montt. This judicial action sends the message that the new Guatemalan government will not tolerate the corrupt practices of the past and that no one is above the law. Also in 2000, the main opposition party, PAN, dissolved in factional disputes. Guatemalan political

observers predict that these developments will lead to new coalitions and perhaps to the formation of additional parties.

New cases of human rights abuse continue to decline, although violence against human rights workers remains a serious challenge. At the same time, violent crime is increasing dramatically. In part, this trend is attributable to economic stagnation and the violent legacy of the war years. The government is taking measures to create new investments in education and job formation. In 2001, the Portillo government increased tax rates to meet the target of increasing the tax burden to 12 percent of GDP. Currently, Guatemala has the lowest tax rates in Central America as well as some of the lowest levels of government per capita expenditures in education and health care.

Faced with these problems, the Portillo government has suggested a national dialogue to open political discussions on the issues. In response, a coalition of civil groups, professional organizations, and private sector interests was formed. This coalition, the Guatemalan Forum, calls for political reforms.

Without economic growth, progress on tax and judicial reform will be slow in coming. Additionally, certain essential elements of the peace plan have not been implemented due to lack of public funds. One important goal of the plan that has been delayed is the expensive and troublesome issue of resettling hundreds of thousands of war refugees still living in Mexico and Honduras and in camps within Guatemala. As Guatemala's leaders make the hard decisions necessary to open the economy to international market forces, they face tensions at home that encourage timidity and a business as usual attitude. With its violent past receding, Guatemala is poised uncertainly to face the future. The country needs, and deserves, courageous leadership to shepherd it into prosperity.

Traditional coffee agriculture requires little initial capital investment and relies on hand labor. This makes it attractive to countries like Guatemala where investment money is scarce and unskilled labor is plentiful. But in a country famous for its plentiful coffee, which sells for $8–12 in the United States, most Mayans drink the dregs of the coffee harvest. They cannot afford to drink the best of the crop they harvest.

CHAPTER

6

Economy

The World Bank classifies Guatemala as a lower middle-income economy. Along with its Central American neighbors who share similar financial circumstances, the country faces a host of challenges to economic prosperity. Overcoming the legacy of the civil war is only the first step in developing a stable economy for the twenty-first century.

After the signing of the peace accord in December 1996, Guatemala seemed to have put many of its past problems to rest. The country's gross domestic product (GDP) for 2001 was approximately $20 billion, and economic growth was 2.3 percent in 2001. Although this is hardly an impressive rate, considering the many obstacles to economic development that Guatemala has faced, it was not a bad one either.

Like other relatively poor countries of the world, Guatemala's modest wealth is based on primary sector economic activities. Primary activities include agriculture, mining, fishing, and forestry. Economies dependent on the primary sector are vulnerable for several reasons. One is that world markets for most agricultural products are highly competitive. Prices fluctuate from year to year, making fiscal planning difficult.

Take coffee, for example, one of Guatemala's main exports. World coffee prices have been in freefall for years. This is due largely to the fact that new producers have entered the market, thus increasing supply. While supplies have grown steadily, demand leveled out more than a decade ago. Prices have fallen accordingly and are not predicted to rise, barring a tremendous natural disaster. Traditional coffee agriculture requires little initial capital investment and relies on hand labor. Both these facts make it an attractive option for developing countries where investment money is scarce and unskilled labor is plentiful. Viet Nam, for example, is one new coffee producer that has increased its output by almost 400 percent over the last ten years, according to the World Bank.

Another reason for vulnerability is that the primary sector, especially agriculture, is subject to weather (such as hurricanes, floods, or droughts), long term-climate change, and various other natural hazards, including disease. A year or two of severe drought can destroy a country's crop. In a diversified economy, the loss of one or two export crops may not make much difference to the overall level of prosperity. But in Guatemala, a ruined coffee crop means that up to half of the country's annual export revenues may be lost. Along with sugarcane and bananas, coffee accounts for almost one-fourth of the total gross domestic product. Almost half of the labor force is engaged in agricultural production, although many farm workers labor in subsistence, rather than export agriculture. A recent example of the fragility of primary sector economies occurred in 1998 when Hurricane Mitch destroyed about 98 percent of Guatemala's banana crop. Nevertheless, Guatemala was lucky compared to Honduras and

El Salvador, both of which lost most of their banana, coffee, and sugarcane crops, as well as much of the infrastructure (highways and power lines, for example) of their countries.

Guatemala has the largest economy in Central America. In 2001, agriculture accounted for 23 percent of gross domestic product (GDP), industry for 20 percent, and the service sector for 57 percent. Agriculture contributes only 23 percent of the GDP, although it accounts for 75 percent of all exports. The steady trend downward in world coffee prices explains in part the slow growth in the post-war years, since so much of export earnings relies on coffee sales to the developed countries. Despite continued reliance on the traditional plantation crops—coffee, bananas, and sugarcane—nontraditional agricultural products such as winter vegetables, fruit, and cut flowers have been growing slowly but steadily in importance.

Other slowly growing sectors that probably will increase in importance in the near future are international tourism, as well as textiles and clothing for the North American market. With the end of the war, Guatemala could capitalize on its spectacular mountain and rainforest scenery, as well as its living Mayan heritage, to attract visitors from the developed countries. Costa Rica, to the south of Guatemala, shares most of the same physical features and has built a thriving eco-tourism economy. Political conditions must be stable and crime must be reduced, however, before tourism can flourish. Assembly manufacturing dominates the industrial sector, and food processing geared to the domestic, U.S., and Central American markets also is important. The United States is the country's largest trading partner, accounting for 27 percent of Guatemala's exports and 35 percent of its imports.

GOING GLOBAL

Since the end of the civil war, Guatemala has moved slowly in the direction of its regional neighbors in creating opportunities for economic growth. Underdeveloped countries dedicated to raising living standards and creating economic choices and freedom have two basic tasks. Although these are simple to state, they both involve complicated political risks and strategies. Eliminating barriers to international trade is one task. Attracting international investment is the other.

In 1998, Guatemala began the process of "going global" in earnest. In that year it passed a foreign investment law to promote direct foreign investment (DFI). Bringing DFI to a less-developed country can be a complicated process, but the benefits tend to outweigh the risks. Worldwide, DFI accounts for far more of the total foreign wealth that goes to poor countries than does official foreign aid. Over the past ten years, in fact, foreign aid from the United States has remained at about the same level—about one-tenth of one percent of GDP! This modest amount is far overshadowed by the amount of private investment dollars flowing from U.S. corporations to those same poor countries.

A common form of DFI is in light assembly plants. For years, corporations based in North America, Europe, and Japan have located facilities for assembling toys, appliances, low-end consumer electronics, clothing, and other items in impoverished countries where unemployment is high and labor is cheap.

Guatemala fits the bill as a suitable site for DFI. Close to the North American market, it can provide quick turnaround times, and its labor rates are competitively low. The new hourly minimum wage is $3.07 in agriculture, $3.38 in industry and construction, and $6.00 for highly skilled labor. Labor unions are legal, but less than 10 percent of the labor force is unionized. Few workers receive health benefits, paid vacations, or pensions from their jobs. The government estimates the formal work force at 3.5 million with at least another million in the informal sector. With an annual population growth rate of 2.5 percent, Guatemala is a young country. Thousands of new workers enter the labor force each year.

These factors combine to make Guatemala an attractive

place to locate a production facility. The features that make Guatemala attractive to U.S. investors, however, also are found in other convenient locations. Therefore, Guatemala must compete with its neighbors for DFI dollars by sweetening the appeal of the country with favorable laws.

One such piece of legislation is Guatemala's Drawback Industry Law. This law is aimed at attracting *maquiladoras*— assembly plants in which at least half of the components and machinery are imported and most of the completed products are exported. The Drawback Law offers a package of incentives to investors that includes a one-year suspension of duties and taxes on imported machinery and a ten-year income tax exemption.

Major U.S. investors in Guatemalan maquiladoras currently include Avon, Bristol-Myers Squibb, Colgate-Palmolive, General Mills, Levi Strauss, Nabisco, and Procter & Gamble. These corporations are engaged in food processing and packaging, cosmetic and over-the-counter drug manufacturing, and clothing assembly. In addition to these investors in the industrial sector, U.S. companies such as Domino's Pizza, Exxon, and McDonald's all have established consumer outlets in Guatemala. Although the effect of these investments on the Guatemalan economy is somewhat less than that provided by the big industrial investors, they nevertheless provide much-needed jobs.

One further obstacle to increasing DFI in Guatemala is shared by most other developing countries. Intellectual property (IP) is not given adequate protection. IP is any product of the intellect that is unique, novel, and has some value in the marketplace. Copyrights, patents, and trademarks are all considered intellectual property. In most developed countries, the legal category of IP also includes inventions, literary creations, brand names, business methods, industrial processes, and chemical formulas. Governments in poorer countries such as Guatemala lack the resources for creating or enforcing effective IP laws, and their courts seem unable to deal with the complexity of international IP cases. To address the issue,

Guatemala passed a new national copyright law in 1998. At about the same time, it signed the Central American Convention on Industrial Property, which recognizes international trademarks and patents, but, again, enforcement is the problem.

Other problems persist, one of which is the lack of a fair and open equities market where shares of public firms are traded. More significantly, foreign investment is restricted in essential security areas and services, such as transportation and airlines. But most sectors are open, and the government is encouraging privatization as a means of bringing in international financing. Privatization also usually means increased efficiency and a savings for government. Recently the Guatemalan postal service was privatized. Plans are underway to partially privatize the state-owned electric company and the national telephone company. Energy development and distribution will be privatized over the next few years. This will mean an increased flow of dollars into the country as the oil fields of Petén are explored and developed. Recently a U.S. company won a 50-year concession to operate the national railroad. All these are healthy signs that the political leadership is moving in the right direction.

Corruption—long a part of the old Guatemalan political economy—is an ongoing concern. If corruption is endemic in a society, it can make business too expensive for foreigners. Bribery is illegal, but it still is practiced commonly. Customs and port officials are notorious for their acceptance of bribes as part of the cost of doing business. Government officials in remote border and rural areas still consider under-the-counter payments a normal part of their jobs. Bribery not only undermines public faith in government, it takes money out of government coffers and discourages foreigners from investing or even visiting certain places.

INTERNATIONAL TRADE AGREEMENTS

As part of the U.S.-Caribbean Basin Initiative, Guatemalan exports receive preferential access to the U.S. market. Through this initiative and other economic programs, the United States hopes to encourage hemispheric trade. As the great North American economic experiment of NAFTA (North American Free Trade Agreement) unfolds, many leaders in the United States and elsewhere are discussing an extension of the agreement to cover more than the three current trading partners—the United States, Canada, and Mexico. For instance, Chile has lobbied to be the first South American member of NAFTA. Chile has worked diligently to meet all the economic and political expectations of the three northern members. Some economic analysts point to the eventual inclusion of the Central American republics in NAFTA as well. In October 1999, Guatemala signed a trade liberalization agreement with Chile, Costa Rica (another early lobbyist for NAFTA membership), El Salvador, Honduras, and Nicaragua. In 2001, a trade agreement with Mexico was formalized. Guatemala is an enthusiastic participant in the regular meetings of the Central American Ministers of Trade. The ministers and trade representatives of five countries meet several times each year to work on regional approaches to trade issues. Guatemala seems determined to enter the global, or at least hemispheric, market as soon as possible.

In a dramatic step, the congress recently passed legislation allowing foreign-currency salaries and bank accounts. International economists view this as an opening for the formal "dollarization" of the Guatemalan economy. Dollarization may take several forms, the most radical of which is called "full dollarization." This happens when a country abandons its own currency and adopts another country's currency (specifically the U.S. dollar) as a means of payment and unit of account. Few countries have accomplished or even attempted full dollarization. Guatemala's Central American neighbor, Panama, fully dollarized several years ago. Given the economic dominance of the United States in the region, it is not too farfetched to imagine Guatemala giving up the quetzal for the greenback in the near future. Dollars already are accepted without question in day-to-day transactions throughout Central America.

In the energy sector, Guatemala is moving into uncharted waters. For a long time, the country has relied upon hydroelectric power, which accounts for 92 percent of its electricity generation. In 1999, however, it became the first Central American country to construct a coal-fired power plant. Guatemala also has several small areas of geothermal potential, although this remains an undeveloped energy source. With the discovery of oil in the Petén, Guatemala becomes the only country in the region apart from Mexico to have a commercial petroleum industry.

In other energy developments, plans are underway to connect the transmission grids of Guatemala, Mexico, and the other Central American countries by the year 2004. Financed by Spain and the InterAmerican Development Bank, this Central American electricity grid will bring a reliable supply of electric power to the region and perhaps beyond. Panama already is linked to Columbia's grid. With the completion of the Central American grid linkage in the next few years, an electric grid that links most of the Western Hemisphere is a possibility in the near future.

While the country's leadership looks forward to a future in which Guatemala is a global economic player, the reality is that the country still is dependent largely on traditional export crops. Coffee is the original moneymaker and it, along with bananas and sugarcane, will continue to be the mainstay of the economy at least for the short term.

Although Guatemala has come far since 1996, high crime rates, high illiteracy rates, and low levels of education hinder further economic growth. Income and wealth distribution is highly skewed. Almost 80 percent of the country's 13 million people live in poverty, and two-thirds of that number live in extreme poverty. The wealthiest 10 percent of the population receive about one-half of all income. Infant mortality and illiteracy rates are among the worst in the hemisphere.

Will Guatemala languish in poverty, or will the new democratic government push its economic reforms forward and raise standards of living? Economic priorities are clear.

The government must support international trade and investment. It must liberalize trade, reform financial services, and overhaul public finances. The tax structure must be simplified, thereby increasing tax compliance, and the tax base must be broadened. These are all steps the government is taking to solve the basic problems. If attempts to increase levels of direct foreign investment (DFI) bear fruit, then taxes will provide more general revenue for education and health, and Guatemala will be positioned to compete better regionally and internationally. It is now up to the people to draw on their heritage of persistence and competition and enter the brave new world of the global marketplace.

Today, the descendents of the old Mayans still live in the highland towns, such as this one near Patzun.

Living in Guatemala Today– Regional Contrasts

G uatemala's cultural diversity is matched with its topograph-
ical variety. Ways of life differ from the sparsely settled Petén
in the north to the highlands and urban areas of the central
mountain ranges, to the Pacific slopes and narrow coastal plain.
Among the country's exotic landscapes, the Sierra Madre highlands
are the most dramatic, both culturally and physically. Here, the way
of life reflects traditions in agriculture, weaving, and trading that
date back to pre-Columbian times.

HIGHLANDS

The Sierra Madre mountain ranges are home to more than
half the country's people. From the very founding of the colony in
the early sixteenth century, the Spanish preferred the cool nights
and relatively mild days of the tierra templada to the choking

humidity and heat of the coastal regions. Successive colonial capitals were built in the region between Guatemala City and Antigua Guatemala, just a few miles to the west. Before the coming of the Europeans, most of the Mayan people likewise settled in the lower elevations of the mountains, even though many of their larger ceremonial cities were located in the flat limestone lands of the Yucatán peninsula. Evidence points to seasonal migrations among the Mayans, who lived in the cool mountains most of the year and traveled to the lower elevations during harvest times.

Today, the descendents of the old Mayans still live in the highlands. The Cakchiquel include about 380,000 people and 6 major dialects. Most live in the area between Antigua Guatemala, the old capital, and Lake Atitlán. Another major group is the Tzutujil to the south and west of Atitlán with 82,000 speakers.

The Quiche Maya live primarily to the north of Atitlán in Quiche department. This is one of the country's largest provinces. It stretches from the Sierra Madre northward across the lower elevations of the Cuchumatanes ranges. The Quiche are the largest linguistic group in Guatemala, numbering approximately 600,000 speakers.

The mid-elevations of the Sierra Madre also are Guatemalan coffee country. In some local areas, almost three out of four agricultural workers labor in the coffee *fincas* (coffee farms). Major coffee-producing departments include Sacatepequez, Guatemala's smallest province, and the much larger department of Esquintla, just to the south. Comprising only 180 square miles (466 square kilometers), Sacatepe-quez nevertheless is well known for its specialty coffees and for the beauty of its provincial capital city, the old town of Antigua Guatemala.

Antigua was the original Spanish capital of Guatemala. Founded in 1541, it was abandoned in 1773 after a tremendous earthquake destroyed most of the city. Years later,

Sixteenth- and seventeenth-century colonial architecture set against a backdrop of volcanic mountains makes Antigua an exotic locale. This seventeenth-century nunnery on the road to Volcán de Agua is still in use.

people began moving back to the town site, and today Antigua is justly famous for its beautiful architecture and dramatic setting. Ruins from the 1773 quake have been incorporated into the urban fabric of the town. Volcán de Agua, which frightened colonial Antiguans in the eighteenth century, now stands dormant on the horizon.

This setting provides a suitable backdrop for Antigua's growing tourist economy. Several large Spanish language schools are located here, as well as many small family operated "language hostels," where foreigners can find modest accommodations and crash courses in Spanish. Picturesque cafes and shops devoted to local crafts cater to the small but steadily growing stream of North American and European tourists who have discovered the area. The town's central plaza, the Parque Centrale, is a traditional colonial town square faced by an old monastery, a church, and government buildings. From Antigua it is only a short drive, or a few hours' hike, into the surrounding mountains and some of the most famous centers of traditional Mayan weaving. During Easter, thousands of Guatemalans converge on Antigua to take part in the elaborate public celebrations.

The highland coffee region extends into Santa Rosa department, to the southeast of Guatemala City and west to another important cultural and physical landmark in Guatemala, Lago de Atitlán. Lake Atitlán long has been a favorite destination for tourists. Surrounded by volcanoes and some of the most traditional Mayan villages in the country, Atitlán lives up to the praise bestowed on it by Aldous Huxley who described it as "the most beautiful place in the world" when he visited it in the 1930s. The shores and slopes of Atitlán are home to 12 small Mayan villages.

Over 12 miles long and 6 miles wide, Atitlán is a large body of water formed when a volcanic eruption and quake dammed up an old 1,000-foot deep volcanic crater, which then slowly filled with water. The lake supported a small commercial fishery for a few years, but overfishing has depleted the stock. Subsistence fishing provides a dietary supplement for some people living in the area. Tiny wooden boats with sharp pointed prows still are used on the lake for fishing and for shoreline travel to and from the villages that

Lake Atitlán has long been a destination for tourists. Today its shores and slopes are home to 12 small Mayan villages.

circle the lake. On the north shore is the village of Panajachel, a destination for European trekkers that has been nicknamed Gringotenango by the locals. Economic analysts and others point out that once the legacy of the long civil war is finally put to rest and the current wave of violent crime abates, then the highlands, especially the Lake Atitlán area, could become a major world tourist attraction.

Not far away, to the northwest of Atitlán, is the famous market town of Chichicastenango. Here, one of the largest Indian markets in Guatemala is held twice weekly, attracting hundreds of buyers and sellers, as well as tourists from the nearby Pan-American Highway. If this major transportation link between the United States and Central America could be upgraded from its present dilapidated state, the infant tourism industry would be given a strong boost.

An efficient modern transportation infrastructure is one of Guatemala's most serious needs. The entire country has fewer than 3,000 miles of paved roads. With the exception of the Pan-American Highway, almost all of the main routes leading through the rural highlands are dirt roads. Even the grand Pan-American route is in many places only a narrow two-lane road with no shoulders, numerous potholes, and an almost total lack of signage.

The southwestern highlands are somewhat different in character from the central Sierra Madre, but the basic lifestyle in this region is the same. Quetzaltenango, Guatemala's second-largest city, is located here. At 7,800 feet (2,377 meters) above sea level, and a population of about 80,000 people, Quetzaltenango is the regional trade and commerce center of the western mountains.

CUCHUMATANES MOUNTAINS

Mayan culture and language also vary in the northern limestone ridges of the Cuchumatanes, but daily life is much the same as it is in the higher Sierra Madres. Principal tribal groups in this remote portion of the country include the Mam, with 450,000 speakers scattered over the border region with Mexico south of the Cuchumatanes; the Kekchi (400,000), who live in the department of Alta Verapaz; and the much smaller Pokomchi tribe, with about 90,000 speakers, in the southern Alta Verapaz.

Subsistence farming, focusing on the staples of corn, beans, squash, and peppers, characterizes the economy of this region. Little coffee is produced here, although coffee fincas in the extreme western department of Huehuetenango and in the central department of Alta Verapaz have increased the area's share of national production over the past several decades.

THE DEPARTMENT OF PETÉN

By far the largest of Guatemala's 22 departments, Petén is the center of Guatemala's oil development as well as home to the country's largest nature reserves. One of Central America's largest areas of contiguous tropical rain forest is located here. The foreign oil companies that are exploring the Petén—Ecuadorean and European—are building a network of roads through the rain forest rapidly. The fear among naturalists working to preserve the Petén's fragile forestlands and among the tourist promoters is that these roads will attract more landless Mayans and others to the region. They are concerned that an increase in the population of this remote region will lead to accelerated deforestation. For years, settlers have been moving in slowly, clearing the forest for subsistence crops or for lands on which to graze cattle.

Petén is also home to Tikal, Uaxactun, El Mirador, Tayasal, and perhaps dozens of other lost cities yet to be discovered and excavated. Currently, tourism is the key industry, but oil development could change that in the years to come.

GUATEMALA CITY

Guatemala City, the primate city known as Guate (pronounced Guat-TAY) by its residents, dominates the country's economic and political life. All of Guatemala's government, banking, and industrial headquarters are located here, along with the main campus of Universidad de San Carlos, the country's first and only public university, and the country's national museums of art and natural history.

Despite its prominence in the life of the country, however, and even though it is located in a mountain basin, Guate lacks the beauty and mystery of the mountains. The biggest city in Central America, it shares none of the attractions that make the rest of the country exotic.

City residents are employed in government or service sectors or, like many of the rural migrants, they are semi-employed in the informal sector in such job categories as street vendors, servants, and market merchants. Estimates are that the informal economic sector employs roughly half of the city's work force. In this regard, as well as in its physical appearance, Guate resembles rapidly growing urban areas in other parts of Latin America. Large new slum neighborhoods are growing in ever expanding rings around the old urban core area. The central business district is noisy and almost always choking with auto exhaust fumes. Street crime in certain neighborhoods is a serious problem, particularly for foreigners unfamiliar with the city's zones. The older part of the city contains some noteworthy nineteenth century architecture, but much of the rest of Guate has a modern look similar to moderately prosperous neighborhoods in North American cities. In keeping with this look, the lifestyle of many of Guate's younger professionals is almost identical to that of educated young people in the United States or Europe. American popular culture is omnipresent, especially clothing, music styles, and entertainment. Guate is in some sense an island of modernity in a sea of traditional Mayan culture.

As the younger generation grows up and out from under the shadow of civil war, life in Guatemala may begin to achieve its potential. This young girl in Chichicastenango carries her sleeping brother in a *tzute*, which is an all-purpose carryall for tortillas, firewood, or babies.

8

Looking Ahead

D espite its problems, Guatemala has many reasons to face the future with optimism. As the civil war recedes in time, and a younger generation grows up without the fear and suspicions of the past, this magnificent land finally may begin to achieve its huge potential.

PROSPECTS FOR ECONOMIC GROWTH

In its response to the end of the civil war, the international community is supporting Guatemala's social and economic objectives. The United States, in particular, has increased its contributions to the country's new program of development projects. Spain, Japan, and other developed countries are supplying money and expertise as well. Much of this funding is dependent upon complete implementation of the peace accords. Still, Guatemala seems fully committed to accomplishing this goal as resources become available.

International financial institutions also are assisting with loans. In April 2002, the International Monetary Fund (IMF) approved a substantial loan program for Guatemala. The World Bank is working to support investments in internationally competitive companies and in tourism. Like other international development funding, these loans are dependent on political reforms. In the case of the IMF, the Guatemalan government has promised to bring about fundamental changes in its financial sector.

Along with the other developing countries of Central America, Guatemala is part of a region that fast is becoming important as a buyer of U.S. goods and services. According to the International Trade Administration, Central America was the eighteenth-largest market for U.S. goods in 2000. This growth in trade is coming at the same time as the benefits of regional trading alliances are becoming apparent to the economic leadership in developing countries. The lessons of the North American Free Trade Agreement are not lost on Guatemala or on other Latin American countries.

In fact, economic regionalization already is developing rapidly in Central America. With the exception of Panama, all the countries of the region have adopted a common external tariff—the first major step toward the creation of a trading union. In addition, the same countries soon will have no internal tariff barriers. This means that goods and services will be able to move freely between the member states. The result almost surely will be increased competition and lower consumer prices for many items. Guatemala, along with Honduras and El Salvador, signed a Free Trade Agreement with Mexico in 2001. Negotiations to establish a Free Trade Agreement of the Americas (FTAA) are planned in 2005. This will be another step toward strengthening regional trade and increasing Guatemala's economic relationship with the United States.

Even apart from the promise of new regional trading alliances, Guatemala is still an excellent market for North America. U.S. companies already enjoy a growing share in the consumer products market. Their exports to Guatemala reached $1.9 billion in 2000. Furthermore, Guatemalans are accustomed to doing business with U.S. firms. Many professional and business people speak English and travel regularly to the United States, which is only three hours away by commercial jet.

Despite the reliance on such vulnerable agricultural commodities as coffee and bananas, the economy grew by 3.3 percent in 2000. New exports, such as clothing, pharmaceuticals, furniture, shrimp, and fresh flowers, are adding to the slow but steady growth in trade. Traditional agricultural production, however, continues to dominate the economy, contributing about 23 percent to the total GDP. The old stigma of the "Banana Republic" lingers here and elsewhere in Central America. Despite government-led efforts to diversify the economy, coffee, sugar, and bananas still account for nearly 50 percent of total exports.

In the realm of future potential economic growth, tourism holds the top position. Even in the face of the setbacks to world tourism since 2001, the tourist industry remains the largest single economic sector of the world's economy. Observers long have commented on the potential for attracting tourists to Guatemala's magnificent scenery, archeological wonders, and living cultural heritage. In this regard, the importance of the end of the civil war cannot be overstated. If Guatemala can continue to implement the peace accords and heal past wounds, it easily might overtake Costa Rica as a first-class eco-tourism destination. Developing eco-tourism would bring in foreign currency and encourage the preservation of natural areas and threatened wildlife. Guatemala could benefit by following the example set by Costa Rica in the 1980s.

EVOLVING POLITICAL LEADERSHIP

Political leadership is a key area of concern for the future. As one of the world's newest democracies, Guatemala is struggling to accept opposing political parties, open elections, universal suffrage, and independent courts—in short, all of the institutions of a democratic society. People in North America and Europe sometimes take for granted the central role these institutions play. The difficulties that new democracies face in establishing them can be daunting. Technically, Guatemala is not a "new democracy"—at least not in the sense that former Soviet republics or new African states are. But for most of its history, and especially for the past 50 years, democracy has existed in name only.

Minor bumps in the road to a prosperous and democratic future are to be expected. For example, many Guatemalans criticized the government of Alfonso Portillo for being anti-business. When President Portillo came into office in January 2000, he threatened to block a number of privatization agreements that had been made by the previous administration. Privatization is the selling off of state-owned industries to the private sector. For much of the twentieth century, socialism or, in the case of Guatemala, authoritarian rule, led governments to own and operate businesses, industries, and services. The belief was that state ownership benefited more people than private ownership did. Over time, however, this belief largely was discredited. State-owned industries became infamous for lack of efficiency and widespread corruption. Selling off state-owned enterprises is a way for developing countries to bring in much needed competition, foreign expertise, and foreign investment. In 1998, the Guatemalan government sold the state-owned telephone company and the electricity distribution company. It also granted a Canadian company a concession to run the national postal service.

Political stability is essential to national development, be it economic or social. In this context, Guatemala has suffered throughout most of its history. Many obstacles must be over-come if conditions are to improve. None is greater or more challenging than narrowing the gap between the country's rich and powerful minority and the poor and powerless majority. This will take time and bold leadership. Tax revenues must be increased, deficit government spending must be reduced, and important public services—such as education and health—must be increased.

Regardless of who sits at the head of government, the country must continue to officially encourage direct foreign investment (DFI). Fortunately, this commitment runs deeper than political party differences. Attracting foreign investment is crucial to economic growth. Although the country moves ahead slowly, bolder leadership quickly might make Guatemala competitive as a DFI magnet. Currently, tax holidays are offered to foreign firms, and there are no restrictions on taking profits out of the country. But these are benefits that foreign companies can find in any number of places in Central America. What Guatemala needs is more money to educate its work force and more money for infrastructure development. Intellectual property rights must be codified in law and accepted in business practices. The currently high rates of violent crime, especially against foreigners, must be stopped. And corruption must be wiped out if real progress is to be made.

Despite these problems, slow progress is evident. For example, a foreign-owned satellite-linked data processing operation employing over 1,400 workers opened recently outside Guatemala City.

DEVELOPING INFRASTRUCTURE

Modernizing the transportation system is a basic step the government should make. Without efficient roads, rail lines, ports, and airfields, Guatemala will not be able to capitalize on its central location in the Western Hemisphere. Guatemalan products, such as fresh cut flowers, already are flown to the United States, Brazil, and Argentina in a few hours. Encouraging the production of other specialty products for quick air shipment to market would spark much needed upgrades to La Aurora International Airport, the country's only world-class airport.

Likewise, the country's three ports need to expand capacity and attract new exports. Bulk products shipped from Guatemalan ports, such as coffee or bananas, can be in the United States within three days. This same quick transit time could be used to ship out any number of value-added products to North America or Europe.

Finding the money to finance port, rail line, and air service upgrades is a critical priority. Neglected for years as the country fought its civil war, Guatemala's antiquated infrastructure has reached the breaking point. To remain competitive with its neighbors, the country must expand its bulk cargo handling facilities. The rail lines linking interior coffee regions with the ports must be improved as well. Currently, most infrastructure development money goes to Guatemala City, rather than to the rail lines in the countryside or to the ports on the Pacific or Atlantic coasts.

The poorly maintained Pan-American Highway linking Guatemala to its northern and southern neighbors is another obstacle to development. Much of Guatemala's economic exchange is with Mexico, Honduras, and El Salvador. But this trade is more expensive than it should be. The Pan-American is unsafe as a major trucking route. In some places, hijackers and bandits can operate without fear of the police. Interregional commerce likely will not increase until the Pan-American is made safe.

Future trends are difficult to predict. As the famous Yogi Berra once said, "Predictions are hard to make, especially about the future." Predictions about Guatemala's future seem especially difficult. With so many interrelated political and economic problems, it seems a place easy to write off as hopeless. A history of mutual suspicion and resentment between ladinos and Mayans seems to point to more of the same in the future.

At the same time, however, Guatemala's people are persistent. They have survived the shocks of colonialism, nightmarish earthquakes, devastating hurricanes, and a civil conflict that scarred two generations. Yet visiting the country today, one finds shyly smiling people in the Mayan villages and optimistic young professionals in Guatemala City. These people seem capable of meeting the challenges of the future, whatever they may be. The land of eternal spring, so long called the land of eternal tyranny, is ready for change. Despite its problems, Guatemala has solid reasons to face the future with hope. As the civil war recedes in time, and a younger generation grows up without the fear and suspicions of the past, this magnificent land finally may live up to its potential.

Guatemala—"Land where the rainbow begins." According to legend, a pot of gold is said to exist at the end (or the beginning) of the rainbow. This Central American country does, indeed, rest upon a metaphorical pot of gold. It is a land of spectacular natural beauty and diversity. It is blessed with a marvelous culture history and a wealth of diverse human resources. For Guatemala and most of its people, however, finding the pot of gold at rainbow's end remains an elusive dream.

Facts at a Glance

Land and People

Official Name	Republic of Guatemala
Location	Middle America, on the Pacific Ocean between Mexico and El Salvador, and the Caribbean Sea between Belize and Honduras.
Area	42,042 square miles (108,890 square kilometers), about the size of Tennessee.
Climate	Tropical, hot lowlands; cool highlands.
Capital	Guatemala City
Other Cities	Quetzaltenango, Puerto Barrios, Champerico, Zacapa, Coban.
Population	13.6 million (2002 estimate)
Major Rivers	Motagua
Mountains	Sierra Madre, Cuchumatanes
Official Language	Spanish (Mayan languages also spoken in rural areas)
Religion	Roman Catholic, Protestant, traditional Mayan.
Literacy rate	63% (2000 estimate)
Average Life Expectancy	66.5

Economy

Natural Resources	Petroleum, nickel, chicle, hydropower
Agricultural Products	Coffee, sugar, bananas, corn, beans, cardamom.
Industries	Textiles, clothing, sugar, furniture, chemicals, rubber, petroleum
Major Imports	Fuels, machinery, construction materials, fertilizers, electricity.
Major Exports	Coffee, bananas, sugar, fruits and vegetables, cardamom, meat, clothing,
Major Trading Partners	United States, Mexico, Japan, El Salvador, Venezuela.
Currency	Quetzal

Government

Form of Government	Constitutional democratic republic
Government Bodies	Executive, legislative, judicial branches
Formal Head of State	President (who is also chief of state)
Voting Rights	18 years of age, universal.

1502   Christopher Columbus sails along eastern shore of Central America on his fourth voyage to the New World.

1523   Spanish enter Guatemalan highlands.

1524   Pedro de Alvarado conquers Guatemala. First Spanish settlement founded near present site of Guatemala City. Captaincy General of Guatemala established.

1541   Antigua founded as administrative center of Captaincy General of Guatemala.

1542   Father Bartolome de Las Casas publishes "A Brief Report on the Destruction of the Indians."

1544   Las Casas named Bishop of Chiapas (Guatemala).

1773   Antigua destroyed by volcanic eruption and subsequent earthquake.

1821   Spain's Central American colonies declare their independence with the Act of September 15, 1821. The Central American Federation, composed of Mexico, Guatemala, El Salvador, Honduras, and Costa Rica, is formed.

1838   Central American Federation formally dissolves.

1840   First coffee farms established.

1873   First coffee exports.

1912   First national railroad links coffee producing areas with ports.

1906   United Fruit Company establishes first banana plantation in Guatemala.

1954   U.S. Central Intelligence Agency backs coup that deposes President Arbenz.

1960   Civil war begins.

1987   Costa Rican President Oscar Arias wins the Nobel Prize for Peace for his Central American Peace Plan. Ending the long Guatemalan civil war is one of Arias's main concerns.

1992   Rigoberta Menchu, Mayan human rights activist, wins Nobel Peace Prize.

1996   Peace Accord signed, ending 36 years of civil war.

Bibliography

Burgos-Debray, Elisabeth, ed. *I . . . Rigoberta Menchu—An Indian Woman in Guatemala.* London: Verso and New Left Books, 1984.

Cameron, Ann, and Thomas Allen. *The Most Beautiful Place in the World.* Random House, 1993.

Harrison, Peter, et. al. *The Lords of Tikal: Rulers of an Ancient Maya City.* London: Thames and Hudson, 1999.

Maslow, Jonathan. *Bird of Life, Bird of Death: A Naturalist's Journey through a Land of Political Turmoil.* New York: Simon and Schuster, 1986.

Sexton, James D. *Mayan Folktales: Folklore from Lake Atitlán, Guatemala.* Anchor, 1992.

Simons, Suzanne, and Diego Isaias Hernandez Mendez. *Trouble Dolls: A Guatemalan Legend.* Scholastic Trade, 2000.

Vecchiato, Gianni. *Guatemala Rainbow.* Pomegranate, 1999.

Websites

CIA World Factbook, Guatemala
  [*http://www.cia.gov/cia/publications/factbook/geos/gt.html*]

U.S. Department of State, Consular General Information Sheet, Guatemala
  [*http://travel.state.gov/guatemala.html*]

U.S. Department of State, Background Note: Guatemala
  [*http://www.state.gov/r/pa/ei/bgn/2045pf.htm*]

agriculture, 10, 16-18, 21-27, 43-45, 48, 57, 65, 66, 70, 76-78, 82, 86, 88, 91, 97
  and Mayans, 38, 39-40, 43, 44-45, 56, 57, 85
airfields, 99, 100
allspice, 24, 25
Alta Verapaz department, 91
altitudinal zonation, 14, 16-18
Alvarado, Pedro de, 42
Amerindians, 10, 19, 21, 23, 29, 32, 34, 35, 54
  See also Mayans
Amnesty International, 68
animal life, 9, 22-23, 27-29
animals, and Mayans, 33, 37-38, 52-53
Antigua Guatemala, 20, 59, 86-88
Arbenz, Jacobo, 65-66
Archbishop's Office for Human Rights (ODHAG), 72
architecture, and Mayans, 31, 32, 34, 38, 39, 53
Arevalo, Juan Jose, 65
Argentina, 100
Aria, Oscar, 68, 70, 71, 72, 73, 75
Armas, Carlos, 66
artisans, and Mayans, 38
assembly manufacturing, 77, 78-79
astronomy, and Mayans, 32, 37
Atitlán, Lake, 9, 20-21, 55, 86, 88, 90
avocado, 28-29
Avon, 79
Aztecs, 29, 32, 34, 40, 42

backstrap loom, 51-52
banana republic, 10, 97
bananas, 10, 16, 44, 76-77, 82, 97, 100
barley, 17
bartering, 38, 57

"battle of the bands," 59
beans, 57, 91
Belize, 14, 22, 24, 68-70
birds, 9, 27-29
Bolivia, 10
borders, 14, 18, 22, 80
  and conflicts, 14, 68-70
Brazil, 100
bribery, 80
Bristol-Myers Squibb, 79
British Honduras, 69
  See also Belize
buses, 61

cactus, 22
Cakchiquels, 47, 86
calendar, and Mayans, 32, 37
Canada, 81, 98
capital cities. See Antigua Guatemala; Ciudad Vieja; Guatemala City
Caribbean lowlands, 21-22
Caribbean Sea, 19, 22
Catholicism, 36, 54-65, 68
cattle, 17, 22, 27, 43
caverns, 22, 55
ceiba tree (yaxche), 52
cenotes (sinkholes), 22
Central American Convention on Industrial Property, 80
Central American Federation (CAF), 43, 64
Central American isthmus, 13, 19
Central American Ministers of Trade, 81
Central American Peace Plan, 68, 70, 71, 72, 73, 75, 95, 97
Champerico, 18
Chiapas, 32
chichicasta plants, 47
Chichicastenango, 54-55, 57, 90
chicle, 24

Index

children
  and infant mortality rate, 48, 82
  and Mayans, 38-39, 47-48, 56-57
Chile, 81
Chuchumantanes Mountains, 29
cinta (Mayan cloth hair ornament), 51
cities, 48, 59-61, 90
  and Mayans, 10, 31, 32, 33-34, 38, 39, 40, 86, 91
  See also capital cities
Ciudad Vieja ("Old Town"), 20
civil war, 10, 49, 65-68, 70-72, 73, 75, 77, 90, 95, 97, 100, 101
civilian defense patrols (PACs), 67
climate/weather, 14, 16-18, 20, 21, 22, 76-77, 85-86, 101
clothing
  for export, 77, 79, 97
  and *ladinos*, 59
  and Mayans, 9, 49-53, 56, 59, 61
cloud forests, 29
coal-fired power plant, 82
cochineal, 43, 44
coffee, 10, 16-17, 21, 44-45, 57, 77, 82, 86, 88, 91, 97, 100
cofradias (religious brotherhoods), 54-55
Cold War, 68
Colgate-Palmolive, 79
colonial period, 20, 21, 29, 32, 40-43, 53, 64, 65, 85-86, 87, 101
color, and Mayans, 37, 49, 52
Columbia, 82
Columbus, Christopher, 40-41, 42
Columbus, Fernado, 40-41
communication, 10, 80, 98
communists, 65-66, 67, 68, 72

Conference on International Trade in Endangered Species (CITES), 24
Congress, 63, 71
Constitutional Court, 63
constitutions, 63-64, 65
Continental Divide, 19
copyright laws, 79-80
corn, 16, 36, 57, 91
corruption, 80, 98, 99
corte (Mayan skirt), 51
Cortéz, Hernan, 42
Costa Rica, 43, 44, 77, 81, 97
coyote, 52
creation myth, and Mayans, 36, 52
crime, 71, 73, 77, 82, 90, 92, 99, 100
Cuchumatanes Mountains, 19, 59, 86, 90-91

dairying, 17
data processing operation, satellite-linked, 99
death squad. *See* White Hand
deforestation, 24, 25-27, 29, 57, 91
democracy, 10, 63, 64, 66, 68, 72, 82, 98
departments, 64
desaparecido (the "disappeared"), 67
dollarization, 81
Domino's Pizza, 79
"Dorado, El," 42
Drawback Industry Law, 79
dress. *See* clothing

earthquakes, 19-20, 39-40, 86, 88, 101
Eastern Coast, 34
economy, 10, 16-18, 24, 25, 29, 38, 43-45, 48, 54-55, 57, 60, 66, 73, 75-83, 88, 90-92, 95-97, 98-101
  See also agriculture

eco-tourism, 27, 77, 97
Ecuador, 91
education, 48, 65, 66, 73, 82, 83,
    92, 99
eggs, 57
El Mirador, 91
El Salvador, 14, 18, 31, 34, 43, 44,
    68, 77, 81, 96
elections, 63, 64, 65, 72, 98
electricity, 80, 82, 98
employment, 48, 73, 79, 92
energy resources, 22, 80, 82, 91,
    98
environmental concerns, 22-27,
    29, 39-40, 70, 91, 97
equator, 14
equities market, 80
erosion, 27
Esquintla department, 86
Europeans, 29, 40-43, 44-45, 53,
    64, 91
    See also Spain
executive branch, 63, 64
exports, 10, 16-17, 21, 24, 25, 44-
    45, 66, 76, 77, 80-81, 82, 97,
    99-100
Exxon, 79

fincas (coffee farms), 86, 91
fishing, 88, 97
flowers, 77, 97, 99-100
food, 16, 36, 57, 88, 91
food processing, 79
forced labor laws, 65
foreign aid, 78, 95-96
foreign currency, 81
foreign investment, 78-80, 83, 96,
    98, 99
forests. *See* tropical rain forests
Free Trade Agreement of the
    Americas (FTAA), 96
Free Trade Agreement, with
    Mexico, 96
fruits, 77
full dollarization, 81

furniture, 24, 97
future, 95-101

General Mills, 79
geothermal power, 82
globalization, 10-11, 77-83, 96
gods, and Mayans, 10, 29, 35, 36,
    53, 55
government, 10, 44, 45, 63-67,
    77, 80, 82-83, 92, 96, 98-99,
    100-101
governors, 64
grazing, 17, 27
Great Britain, and Belize, 68-70
gross domestic product (GNP),
    75, 76, 77, 97
Guatemala City (Guate), 19, 20,
    42, 58, 59-61, 66, 86, 88, 92-93,
    100, 101
Guatemalan Forum, 73
Guatemalan Labor Party, 65-66, 66
Guatemalan Republican Front
    (FRG), 71, 72
Guerrilla Army of the Poor, 66
guerrilla groups, 66-67, 70
Gulf of Honduras, 22

haab (Mayan solar year), 36-37
haggling, 39, 57
hardwoods, 23
health care, 48, 66, 73, 78, 83, 99
highlands, 19-21, 33, 34, 47-59, 67,
    85-88, 90
Historical Clarification Commission
    (CEH), 72
history, 9-10, 20, 21, 29, 31-45, 32,
    40-43, 53, 64-68, 85-86, 87, 101
    See also Mayans
holidays, 88
Honduras, 14, 22, 31, 33, 41, 43,
    44, 68, 73, 76-77, 81, 96
horses, and Spain, 42, 53
housing, and Mayans, 57
Huehuetenango department,
    91

Index

huipil (Mayan blouse), 49-50, 51, 52

human rights, 51, 67, 68, 70-71, 72, 73

Hurricane Mitch, 76-77

hurricanes, 76-77, 101

Huxley, Aldous, 9, 20, 21, 88

hydroelectric power, 82

I, Rigoberta Menchu, An Indian Woman in Guatemala, 67

imports, 24, 77, 96, 97

income inequality, 48, 57, 82, 99

independence, 43-45, 64

industries, 43, 77, 78-79, 80, 98

infant mortality rate, 48, 82

informal economic sector, 92

intellectual property protection, 79-80, 99

Inter-American Commission on Human Rights of the Organization of American States, 68

InterAmerican Development Bank, 82

International Monetary Fund (IMF), 96

International Network of Biosphere Reserves, 23

Izabal, 66

Japan, 95

judicial branch, 63, 64, 73, 98

karst topography, 22

katun (Mayan number set), 37

Kekchi, 91

La Aurora International Airport, 100

labor force, 76, 78, 86, 92, 99

labor unions, 65-66, 78

ladinos, 10, 54, 58, 59-61, 101

land reforms, 65, 66, 70

land rights, 44-45, 64, 68

"land where the rainbow begins," 9, 11, 49, 101

language hostels, 88

languages, 47, 52, 53-54, 59, 86, 88, 90, 91

laterization, 25-27

latitude, 14

legislative branch, 63, 71

Levi Strauss, 79

location, 13, 14, 99

lower middle-income economy, 75

lowlands. *See* Caribbean lowlands; Pacific lowlands

lumber, 24

McDonald's, 79

magic, and Mayans, 37-38

mahogany, 24

Mam, 91

mangrove swamps, 18

manioc, 26-27

maquiladoras (assembly plants), 79

marimba, 58-59

market towns, 38, 54-55, 57, 90

Maya Biosphere Reserve (MBR), 22-25, 91

Mayans
  and agriculture, 38, 39-40, 43, 44-45, 56, 57, 85, 91
  and architecture, 31, 32, 33, 34, 38, 39, 53
  and astronomy, 32, 37
  and body decorations, 38-39
  and chicle, 25
  and children, 56-57
  and cities, 10, 31, 32, 33-34, 38, 39, 40, 86, 91
  and civil war, 66, 67-68, 70, 72
  and clothing, 9, 49-53, 56, 61
  and cultural timeline, 32
  and daily life, 47-59, 85, 90
  and decline of classic culture, 39-40

and elections, 72
and Europeans, 29, 41, 42, 43, 44-45, 53, 64
and food, 57, 91
history of, 9, 10, 31-40, 86
and housing, 57
and human rights, 67, 68, 70
and invasion by other groups, 32, 40
ladinos versus, 101
and languages, 47, 53-54, 86, 90, 91
and migration to Guatemala City, 51, 60
and music, 58-59
and numerology, 32, 36-37
and Petén ruins, 23
population of, 10
and religion, 9, 10, 27-29, 33-40, 51-56
and settlement patterns, 85-88, 90-91
and social structure, 38-39, 40
and time, 32, 36-37
and trade, 54-55, 57, 85, 90
and weaving, 49-53, 56, 57, 85, 88
and women, 49-53
mayors (councils), 64
Mein, John Gordon, 67
Menchu, Rigoberta, 51, 67, 68
Menchu Foundation, 71
merchants, and Mayans, 38
Mesoamerica, 33
Mexican Empire, 64
Mexico, 14, 18, 24, 32, 42, 43, 73, 81, 82, 91, 96
Mexico City, 42
military dictatorships, 10, 64, 66-68, 71-72, 73, 98
minimum wage, 78
modernism, 10
    and Guatemala City, 60-61, 92-93
    and Resplendent Quetzal, 9, 27-29

Motagua River, 19, 22
Motagua Valley, 22, 34
mountains, 14, 16, 17-18, 19-21, 22, 29, 55, 56, 59, 85-88, 90-91
municipalities, 64
museums, 92
music, 58-59

Nabisco, 79
NAFTA (North American Free Trade Agreement), 81, 96
national symbol. *See* Resplendent Quetzal
natural landscapes, 9, 10, 13-14, 16-29, 55, 56, 59, 85-88, 90-91, 101
natural resources, 22, 24, 80, 82, 91
nature reserve, 22-25, 91
Nicaragua, 43, 44, 68, 81
Nobel Peace Prize
    to Aria, 68
    to Menchu, 51, 68
numerology, and Mayans, 32, 36-37

ocean currents, 18
Ocos, 18
October Revolutionaries, 65
Olmecs, 34
Organization of Guatemalan National Revolutionary Unity (URNG), 67, 70
ox cart roads, 44

Pacaya volcano, 19
Pacific lowlands, 10, 14, 16, 85
Pacific Ocean, 19
Pacific "Ring of Fire," 19
Palenque, 34
PAN, 72
Panajachel (Gringotenago), 90
Panama, 82, 96
Pan-American Highway, 90, 100

patents, 79-80
peacocks, and Spain, 53
peppers, 57, 91
Petén, 22-25, 80, 82, 85, 91-93
petroleum, 22, 80, 82, 91
pharmaceuticals, 79, 97
plant life, 9, 18, 22-27, 28-29
    See also tropical rain forests
plantations, 16-17, 65, 77
    See also bananas; coffee; sugar-
        cane
Pliocene, 13
Pokomchi tribe, 91
political parties, 65-66, 71, 72-73,
    98, 99
Popol Vuh, 36, 51
population, 10, 19, 47-48, 78
Portillo, Alfonso, 71, 72, 73, 98
ports, 10, 18, 21, 44, 80, 99, 100
postal service, 89, 98
potatoes, 17
poverty, 48, 60, 82, 92
president, 63, 64
prickly pear cacti, 44
priests, and Mayans, 36-37, 38,
    40
primary sector economic activities,
    76
primate city, 60, 92
    See also Guatemala City
privatization, 80, 98
Procter & Gamble, 79
Puerto Barrios, 21
pyramids. *See* ziggurats

quetzal (bird). *See* Resplendent
    Quetzal
quetzal (currency), 29, 81
Quetzalcoatl (Plumed Serpent),
    10, 29, 35, 53
Quetzaltenango, 59, 90
Quiche department, 86
Quiche Maya, 36, 51, 86
Quirigua, 34

railroads, 10, 44, 66, 80, 99, 100
rainfall, 18, 22
Rebel Armed Forces, 66
regional security, 14, 68-70
regions, 85-88, 90-93
religion, 36, 54
    and Mayans, 9, 10, 27-29, 33-40,
        51-56
Resplendent Quetzal, 9, 27-29
Revolutionary Organization of
    Armed People, 66
Rios Montt, Efrain, 71-72
roads, 22, 44, 47, 90, 91, 99
roof combs, 33

Sacatepequez department, 86-88
"sacral society," 34-38
San Antonio Aguas Calientes,
    47
San Jose, 18
Santa Maria volcano, 19
Santa Rosa department, 88
sapodilla tree. *See* chicle
Sarstun, Rio, 22
Secret Anti-Communist Army
    (ESA), 67
service economic sector, 77
settlement patterns, 16, 19, 20,
    21, 86
shrimp, 97
Sierra Madre Mountains, 17, 19,
    20, 49, 85-88, 90
size, 10, 14
slash-and-burn shifting agriculture,
    23, 25-27, 39
slums, 60, 92
snow, 17
social security system, 65
social structure, 38-39, 40, 48
Spain, 20, 21, 32, 44, 53, 64, 65,
    82, 85-86, 87, 95, 101
Spanish language, 53-54, 59, 88
squash, 91
stick houses, 57

stratovolcanoes, 19, 20
subsistence agriculture, 16, 17, 22, 23, 25-27, 38, 39-40, 43, 76, 91, 97
sugarcane, 10, 16, 18, 43, 76, 77, 82, 97
Supreme Court, 63, 72
sustainable agriculture, 23-25
swamps, 18
syncretism, 36, 54-56

Tabasco, 32
Tajumulco, 18
tariffs, 96
taxation, 73, 83, 96, 99
taxis, 61
Tayasal, 91
telegraph lines, 10, 66
telephone company, 98
temples, and Mayans, 33, 39
textiles, for export, 77
    See also clothing; weaving
tierra caliente ("hot land"), 16, 21
Tierra del Fuego, 19
tierra fria ("cold land"), 16, 17
tierra helado ("frozen land"), 16, 17-18
tierra templada ("temperate land"), 16-17, 47, 85
Tikal, 31, 32, 34, 91
time, and Mayans, 32, 36-37
Toltecs, 32, 34, 35, 40
tortillas, 57
total fertility rates (TFR), 47-48
tourism, 27, 77, 88, 90, 91, 96, 97
trade, 10, 16-18, 21, 24, 25, 38, 44-45, 54-55, 57, 76, 77, 78, 80-83, 85, 90, 96-97, 99-100
trademarks, 79-80
trading union, 96
tradition, 10, 11, 85
    and Guatemala City, 60-61, 93
    and Resplendent Quetzal, 9, 27-29
    See also Mayans

traje (Mayan costume), 9, 49-53, 61
transportation, 10, 22, 43, 44, 47, 61, 66, 80, 90, 91, 99-100
tropical rain forests, 9, 14, 22-27, 23-25, 48, 91
tropics. See climate/weather
tun (Mayan drum), 59
tzicolai (Mayan flute), 59
tzolkin (Mayan time unit), 36-37
tzute (Mayan all-purpose carryall), 51
Tzutujils, 86

Uaxactun, 91
Ubico, Jorge, 65
unemployment, 60
United Fruit Company (El Pulpo, the Octopus), 10, 66
United Nations (UN), 70, 71
United Provinces of Central America. See Central American Federation
United States, 10, 24, 25, 66-68, 77, 78, 79, 80-81, 90, 92-93, 95, 96-97, 100
U.S. Central Intelligence Agency (CIA), 66
U.S.-Caribbean Basin Initiative, 80-81
universal suffrage, 98
Universidad de San Carlos, 92
Usumacinta Valley, 34

vegetables, 77
Volcán Atitlán, 20
Volcán de Agua, 20, 87
Volcán San Pedro, 20
Volcán Tolimán, 20
volcanoes, 9, 10, 17, 18, 19, 20-21, 22, 40, 55, 87

war refugees, 70, 73
warriors, and Mayans, 38

Index

water features, 9, 19, 20-24, 55, 86, 88, 90
weaving, and Mayans, 49-53, 56, 57, 85, 88
wheat, 16
White Hand (death squad), 67, 70-71, 72
women
  and elections, 72
  and Mayans, 39, 49-53, 56

workers, and Mayans, 39, 40
World Bank, 75, 96

xate ferns, 24, 25

yams, 26-27
Yucatán Peninsula, 22, 32, 33, 86

Zacapa, 66
ziggurats, and Mayans, 33, 39, 53

Picture Credits

page:

8:	Roger E. Dendinger	50:	Roger E. Dendinger
11:	© 2003 maps.com	53:	KRT/NMI
12:	New Millennium Images	55:	Reuters Photo Archive/NMI
15:	© 2003 maps.com	56:	Roger E. Dendinger
16:	Roger E. Dendinger	58:	Roger E. Dendinger
17:	Roger E. Dendinger	60:	Roger E. Dendinger
21:	Roger E. Dendinger	62:	AFP/NMI
23:	New Millennium Images	69:	AFP/NMI
26:	© Kennan Ward/CORBIS	71:	AFP/NMI
28:	© Michael & Patricia Fogden/CORBIS	74:	Zuma Press/NMI
30:	New Millennium Images	84:	New Millennium Images
35:	AFP/NMI	87:	Roger E. Dendinger
41:	AFP/NMI	89:	Roger E. Dendinger
46:	Roger E. Dendinger	94:	Roger E. Dendinger

Cover: © Dave Houser/CORBIS

115

About the Author

ROGER E. DENDINGER was born in New Orleans and grew up there and in Mobile, Alabama. He is an associate professor of geography at the South Dakota School of Mines and Technology in Rapid City, South Dakota. In addition to teaching and writing, he enjoys hiking and fishing in the central Black Hills where he lives with his wife, Amy, and their three sons, Zac, Nash, and Gabe. Among his research travels, he spent a summer doing field work in the Guatemalan highlands.

CHARLES F. ("FRITZ") GRITZNER is Distinguished Professor of Geography at South Dakota State University in Brookings. He is now in his fifth decade of college teaching and research. During his career, he has taught more than 60 different courses, spanning the fields of physical, cultural, and regional geography. In addition to his teaching, he enjoys writing, working with teachers, and sharing his love for geography with students. As consulting editor for the MODERN WORLD NATIONS series, he has a wonderful opportunity to combine each of these "hobbies." Fritz has served as both president and executive director of the National Council for Geographic Education and has received the Council's highest honor, the George J. Miller Award for Distinguished Service.